Robert Lee Frost ... ... 1874. When he wa. ... ... his mother moved to New England. He attended school at Dartmouth and Harvard, worked in a mill, taught, and took up farming before he moved to England, where his first books of poetry, *A Boy's Will* (1913) and *North of Boston* (1914), were published. *North of Boston* brought him recognition as the preeminent voice of New England and as one of America's major poets. In 1915 he returned to the United States and settled on a farm in New Hampshire. Four volumes of his poetry—*New Hampshire* (1923), *Collected Poems* (1930), *A Further Range* (1936), and *A Witness Tree* (1942)—were awarded the Pulitzer Prize. He died in 1963.

William H. Pritchard is Professor of English at Amherst College and the author of *Randall Jarrell: A Literary Life, Frost: A Literary Life Reconsidered*, and *Lives of the Modern Poets*.

Peter Davison is the author of ten books of verse, culminating in *The Poems of Peter Davison, 1957–1996*, as well as a memoir, *Half Remembered: A Personal History*; a book of criticism, *One of the Dangerous Trades: Essays on the Work and Working of Poetry*; and a literary chronicle, *The Fading Smile: Poets in Boston from Robert Frost to Robert Lowell to Sylvia Plath, 1955–1960*. He is also poetry editor of *The Atlantic Monthly*.

POEMS BY ROBERT FROST

A Boy's Will

and

North of Boston

INTRODUCTION BY
WILLIAM H. PRITCHARD

WITH A NEW AFTERWORD BY
PETER DAVISON

A SIGNET CLASSIC

SIGNET CLASSIC
Published by New American Library, a division of
Penguin Putnam Inc., 375 Hudson Street,
New York, New York 10014, U.S.A.
Penguin Books Ltd, 27 Wrights Lane,
London W8 5TZ, England
Penguin Books Australia Ltd, Ringwood,
Victoria, Australia
Penguin Books Canada Ltd, 10 Alcorn Avenue,
Toronto, Ontario, Canada M4V 3B2
Penguin Books (N.Z.) Ltd, 182–190 Wairau Road,
Auckland 10, New Zealand

Penguin Books Ltd, Registered Offices:
Harmondsworth, Middlesex, England

Published by Signet Classic, an imprint of New American Library,
a division of Penguin Putnam Inc.

First Signet Classic Printing, January 1990
First Signet Classic Printing (Davison afterword), April 2001

20 19 18 17 16 15 14 13 12 11

 REGISTERED TRADEMARK—MARCA REGISTRADA

Library of Congress Catalog Card Number: 00-049651

Printed in the United States of America

CONTENTS

CONTENTS

INTRODUCTION

A Boy's Will, Robert Frost's first book of poetry, was published in March 1913, a week or so after his thirty-ninth birthday; *North of Boston*, his second book, appeared a little over a year later. What is striking about these two events, marking the brilliant debut of a poet we now think of as quintessentially American, is not only Frost's advanced age as he makes his first poetic bows, but also the fact that they happened in England. He had gone there with his wife and four children in the fall of 1912, having made a dramatic departure from the life of farming and of teaching in which he had been engaged for more than a decade. Although a few of his poems had appeared in American magazines and newspapers, Frost felt that his success was too modest to justify any attempt at publishing a volume. Yet—and surprisingly—soon after settling in England, he proceeded to assemble the contents of a slim book and carry it with him down to London, where he placed it with a small English publisher of some quality, David Nutt. Writing in November 1912 to Thomas Mosher, an American publisher who had expressed interest in printing a book of his poems, Frost confessed that *A Boy's Will* was already contracted for, although he took pains to insist on the unforeseen, unplanned nature of the event: "I brought [the manuscript] to England in the bottom of my trunk, more afraid of it, probably, than the Macnamara of what he carried in his. I came here to write rather than to publish." Such insistence on the randomness with which things happened was part of a larger pattern in Frost's thinking about poetry and life, particularly the insistence that "wholly on impulse" (as he described his taking *A Boy's Will* to David Nutt) are the most significant and consequential acts performed.

Frost had his doubts about whether publishing this first book of poems in England was a prudent thing to do, asking in one of his letters home if it wouldn't seem "traitorously un-American to have all my first work come out over here." Such doubts were momentarily assuaged by the rapidity with which he made new literary acquaintances, most important the English poet F. S. Flint and—through Flint's suggestion— the American poet and publicist Ezra Pound, both of whom would review *A Boy's Will.* Through Pound, Frost also met W. B. Yeats, who had good words for the book although (as Frost's wife, Elinor, noted regretfully) he did not express them in print. But Frost was not about to be too quickly or easily satisfied by the achievement of having gotten his work published. For one thing, he wrote to Mosher, he had "three other books of verse somewhere near completion," and thus could afford, so it seemed, to be slightly detached from his first volume. In a letter written before moving to England, he had said dryly that neither "My November Guest" nor "Reluctance," two of the best poems in *A Boy's Will,* heralded "a new force in literature." "Indeed," he went on, "I think I have others still under cover that more nearly represent what I am going to be." By these "others" Frost meant the "speech" poems—the dramatic monologues and dialogues which, in *North of Boston,* would consolidate and diversify the achievement of *A Boy's Will.*

"How can they help seeing how exquisitely beautiful some of the poems are, and what original music there is in most of them?" wrote Elinor Frost to a friend in America. By this time—early July 1913—

there had been a few English reviews of *A Boy's Will* (it would not be published in America until 1915), but in the main they dwelt on the poems' "simplicity," as if their author were guileless. Pound's review of the book, which appeared in September, found it to possess "utter sincerity," but he also managed to patronize *A Boy's Will*: "a little raw, and has in it a number of infelicities; underneath them it has the tang of the New Hampshire woods"—a tang that Pound doesn't convince us he's experienced. Rather than being called simple, sincere, and "raw," Frost would have preferred that reviewers notice the subtlety of at least some of the poems in his first book: "You are not going to make the mistake that Pound makes," he wrote Mosher, "of assuming that my simplicity is that of the untutored child. I am not undesigning."

In some of the poems in *A Boy's Will*, the design was uncomplicated and the rhythmic figure straightforward—as here in the first stanza of "Going for Water":

> The well was dry beside the door,
>   And so we went with pail and can
> Across the fields behind the house
>   To seek the brook if still it ran; . . .

Another poem, "In a Vale," has a lilting "poetical" swing such as would be familiar to any reader of late nineteenth-century English or American verse:

> When I was young, we dwelt in a vale
>   By a misty fen that rang all night,
> And thus it was the maidens pale
> I knew so well, whose garments trail
>   Across the reeds to a window light.

Even the final poem in *A Boy's Will*, "Reluctance," which a number of readers had already admired, was unsurprising in its tune and rather insistent in its rhyming:

Ah, when to the heart of man
  Was it ever less than a treason
To go with the drift of things,
  To yield with a grace to reason,
And bow and accept the end
  Of a love or a season?

But in other poems Frost had begun to experiment successfully with more subtle rhythms and tones of voice that created "original music" (in Elinor Frost's words) by playing off the rhythms of speech—and it was more often speech than song—against the circumstances of meter, rhyme, and stanza. What he first referred to, in an important letter of July 4, 1913, as "the sound of sense," was something distinct from, even in opposition to "the harmonized vowels and consonants" that recent masters like Swinburne and Tennyson had made into "the music of poetry."

Frost's different music was made, by contrast, out of "the sound of sense," and in a poem such as "Mowing" he had, in his own words, "come so near what I long to get that I almost despair of coming nearer." But another poem from the volume, "Storm Fear," demonstrates just as strikingly what he had in mind:

When the wind works against us in the dark,
And pelts with snow
The lower chamber window on the east,
And whispers with a sort of stifled bark,
The beast,
'Come out! Come out!'—
It costs no inward struggle not to go,
Ah, no!
I count our strength,
Two and a child,
Those of us not asleep subdued to mark
How the cold creeps as the fire dies at length,—
How drifts are piled,

Dooryard and road ungraded,
Till even the comforting barn grows far away
And my heart owns a doubt
Whether 'tis in us to arise with day
And save ourselves unaided.

"Storm Fear" is a poem that some readers of *A Boy's Will* might have thought of as simple; after all, there are only two words of more than two syllables in the whole of it, while the feeling of helplessness and fear is an easily available one. Indeed the poem's named circumstances are as familiar, even as comforting, as the barn used to be until the snow made it seem far away. But one is soon struck by how the disposition of words, of line lengths and rhymes, is not simple at all. It is the expressive use of materials that makes the poem's overall pace so interesting and satisfying: consider, for example, the way the short line "Two and a child" sounds and looks like not much protection when compared with "How the cold creeps and the fire dies at length"—a line that takes as long to say as it did to feel the creeping cold and dying fire. The rhymes create continuity and suppleness of movement by never quite coming when you expect them; by having the last word of the line "Those of us not asleep subdued to mark" rhyme with the ends of lines much earlier in the poem; by having the key word "doubt" in the third from the last line go all the way back to rhyme with the early "Come out!"; by deferring, over the course of five lines, such an ingenious rhyming pair of words as "ungraded" and "unaided." In a phrase from Milton's preface to *Paradise Lost*, the poem's "sense" is "variously drawn out from one verse into another." A sequence such as "Till even the comforting barn grows far away/ And my heart owns a doubt/ Whether . . ." anticipates the even more daring drawings-out of sense Frost was already making in the *North of Boston* poems he was soon to publish.

In an attempt to provide continuity for the poems in *A Boy's Will*, Frost wrote short glosses after the title of nearly every one, so as to suggest that the book had a story of sorts. In that story, a young man chooses solitude and the privacy of dreams (the gloss for "Into My Own," the volume's opening poem, is "The youth is persuaded that he will be rather more than less himself for having forsworn the world"), but eventually, in "Mowing," "He takes up life simply with the small tasks." There is also a seasonal cycle— from one autumn to the next—to complement the personal cycle. The poems don't really need or in some cases even justify the glosses, and though they have a certain charm, Frost dropped them later on. But in distancing himself, the author of *A Boy's Will*, from the "youth" who was exercising that will (in Longfellow's poem "My Lost Youth" the refrain sings that "A boy's will is the wind's will, / And the thoughts of youth are long, long thoughts"), Frost wanted to show he was no callow romantic. After the book was published, he said of it that "The beauty of such things as 'Into My Own,' 'My November Guest,' 'A Dream Pang,' 'Mowing,' and 'Reluctance' is that they are not just postgraduate work, nor post-postgraduate work, but the unforced expression of a life I was forced to live." That "life" that the man, Frost, was "forced to live" has, in the poems, been handed over to the youth, while the poet's expression of that life is free, "unforced" in the subtlety and beauty of its music. So, in the lovely "October," as (in the words of the gloss) the youth "sees days slipping from him that were the best for what they were," the poet bids to enchant the October morning with lines like these:

> Make the day seem to us less brief.
> Hearts not averse to being beguiled,
> Beguile us in the way you know;
> Release one leaf at break of day;

> At noon release another leaf;
> One from our trees, one far away;
> Retard the sun with gentle mist;
> Enchant the land with amethyst.
> Slow, slow!

The last line beautifully enacts the retard being called for, however oblivious the October morning may be to such entreaties.

Frost's claim that he was "not undesigning" was, if anything, a designed understatement. For as soon as *A Boy's Will* was published in England, he began to contrive—with his friend and ex-student John Bartlett, now living in Vancouver—to publicize the book in America. Care was to be taken not to offend American editors and publishers by emphasizing (as Pound had emphasized in his review) that Frost had to move to England in order to get published. There was also revealed a most specific plan for the book that was to follow hard on the heels of *A Boy's Will*; that book was to be of a different cast and style. As he wrote to Mosher, "If I write more lyrics it must be with no thought of publication. What I *can* do next is bring out a volume of blank verse that I have already well in hand." He went on to characterize the new style as follows: "I had some character strokes I had to get in somewhere and I chose a sort of eclogue form for them. Rather I dropped into that form. And I dropped to an everyday level of diction that even Wordsworth kept above." As usual, Frost's effort was an inclusive one, dedicated to making an impact on as many readers, both English and American, as he could: "I want to be a poet for all sorts and kinds," he wrote Bartlett in November 1913. "I want to reach out, and would if it were a thing I could do by taking thought." Even more grandly, he confided to Bartlett that he expected "to do something to the present state of literature in America."

Unlike the quiet, sometimes rather old-fashioned lyrics from his first volume, the poems in what was eventually titled *North of Boston* (earlier projected titles included "Farm Servants and Other People," "New England Eclogues," and "New England Hill Folk") would reach out to "all sorts and kinds."

This new book of mainly blank verse—which, in July 1913, he said he had already "well in hand"— was probably substantially completed before Frost sailed for England; and in his important study of the years in England, John Evangelist Walsh has argued persuasively that the months previous to Frost's departure were a time of creative ferment on his part (*Into My Own: The English Years of Robert Frost,* 1988). The impulse, then, to theorize about "the sound of sense"—an impulse that reached its peak in the summer of 1913 and continued on into 1914—was an attempt to rationalize what he had done in the *North of Boston* poems about to be published (the book appeared in May 1914). Surely Frost must have had some misgivings and uncertainties about poems like "The Death of the Hired Man," or "Home Burial," or "A Servant to Servants." To have dropped to a level of diction even Wordsworth "kept above" was to risk from the critics the kinds of condescension and disbelief similar to those that greeted Wordsworth's publication of the *Lyrical Ballads.* Like his great predecessor, Frost's attempt was to "choose incidents and situations from common life, and to relate or describe them throughout, as far as possible in a selection of language really used by men." (So Wordsworth wrote, in his 1800 Preface to the *Lyrical Ballads.*) But in one way Frost's experiment was even more radical than Wordsworth's insofar as he did not only or always "relate and describe" common incidents and situations. He also suppressed or downplayed the narrative line by making it consist of no more or less than a voice, or voices, in conflict with itself, or with other

voices. So the woman who speaks in "A Servant to
Servant" sounds like this:

> It seems to me
> I can't express my feelings any more
> Than I can raise my voice or want to lift
> My hand (oh, I can lift it when I have to).
> Did ever you feel so? I hope you never.
> It's got so I don't even know for sure
> Whether I *am* glad, sorry, or anything.
> There's nothing but a voice-like left inside
> That seems to tell me how I ought to feel,
> And would feel if I wasn't all gone wrong.

There is no narrative presence here in the form of a
poet who, in due time, will intrude and tell us what
the woman is "really" feeling or suffering. At the end
of perhaps the most agonized of these poems, "Home
Burial," the grief-stricken wife hurls at her husband
the following charge: "*You*—oh, you think the talk is
all." But in a sense he's right, since in dialogue like
"Home Burial" the talk really *is* all. Only through
such talk are "characters" made and perceived.

"The living part of a poem is the intonation entan-
gled somehow in the syntax idiom and meaning of a
sentence. It is only there for those who have heard it
previously in conversation." Frost wrote those words
to his American friend and disciple Sidney Cox in
early 1914, going on to insist: "Words exist in the
mouth, not in books. You can't fix them and you don't
want to fix them." The passage from "A Servant to
Servants" quoted above is compelling in its un-
fixedness; in the way the woman's voice expresses it-
self over the blank verse lines in sentences, irregular
in length, that contrast vividly with themselves. (Con-
sider the difference between the lengthy opening sen-
tence, with its parenthetical close, and the vivid
homely force of "I hope you never.") It is, first and

perhaps last—though not merely—the sentence-sounds that interested Frost. He once claimed it was not until writing "The Death of the Hired Man" that he discovered he was interested in more than merely his neighbors' tones of speech. But this acknowledgment of a "human interest" additional to speech only suggests how strong for him were speech's claims and charms. One of his best formulations on the subject was made in a letter to Bartlett, some months prior to *North of Boston*'s appearance, when he insisted that "*The ear does it.* The ear is the only true writer and the only true reader." "The best part of what a good writer puts into his work" was what mere eye-readers missed. "We must imagine the speaking voice," he put it most succinctly, and that speaking voice was different from the intoning one he had often employed in *A Boy's Will*: "One thing to notice is that but one poem in [*North of Boston*] will intone and that is 'After Apple-Picking.' The rest talk."

The "talk" in *North of Boston* begins—or began, in the book as published in 1914—with Frost's little poem "The Pasture," printed in italics as a sort of epigraph to the volume. *"I sha'n't be gone long—You come too"* was its repeated colloquial invitation, really an invitation to listen. But listen is what one must do if one is to take in the speaking voice that performs in the remarkable opening poem of the book, "Mending Wall." The poem's theme—the appropriateness of building barriers such as stone walls between human beings or their landed properties—is familiar enough. But only a listener can catch such an effect as occurs in the following lines, early in the poem, when the narrator is at pains to distinguish the kind of holes, or gaps in the wall, which he and his neighbor set about each year to mend:

The work of hunters is another thing:
I have come after them and made repair

> Where they have left not one stone on a stone,
> But they would have the rabbit out of hiding,
> To please the yelping dogs. The gaps I mean,
> No one has seen them made or heard them made, . . .

The careless hunters' actions are set forth in a hurried, rather pell-mell rush of words ("Where they have left not one stone on a stone") that finally concludes itself with "the yelping dogs." A pause in the middle of the line, then an unmistakable speech inflection: "The gaps I mean, /No one has seen them made or heard them made." Here the word "I" must take a strong accent, by way of distinguishing these gaps from the gaps he doesn't mean, even as he has just devoted some lines to describing those latter ones. "Never if you can help it," Frost wrote to Bartlett, "write down a sentence which doesn't posture specially." Much of the pleasure and vividness in "Mending Wall" and the other poems in *North of Boston* consist in the accurate registration of special postures of speech, and through them the further tones and nuances Frost wants to give us.

Yet it would be a mistake to take him too much at his word and assume that *North of Boston* was written wholly and solely at the "low" speech and diction level even Wordsworth kept above. In "Mending Wall" there is an easy intimacy of talk, sometimes verging on the folksy, as when the narrator wants to ask about his neighbor—the stubborn farmer who believes and reasserts that "Good fences make good neighbours"—"Why do they make good neighbours? Isn't it/Where there are cows? But here there are no cows." But near the poem's end the narrator's voice rises to a higher and rather more mysterious level of assertion, as he presents the farmer-neighbor once more:

> I see him there
> Bringing a stone grasped firmly by the top
> In each hand, like an old-stone savage armed.

He moves in darkness as it seems to me
Not of woods only and the shade of trees.

This darkness may be something more than benighted-
ness, and may even call forth an admiring wonder on
the part of the "enlightened" narrator; at any rate,
the special posture of the lines just quoted is less dis-
tinct, more evocative, and more stirring than are the
colloquial postures against which it is played off. Frost
knew that in writing poems on a single level of dic-
tion—a fairly unelevated one—he ran the risk of mo-
notony, exactly the fate literature had at all costs to
avoid.

So at crucial moments in the poems in which the
narrator or one of the speaking characters makes a
discovery, or expresses a thought that had hitherto
been harbored up inside, the verse become corres-
pondingly elevated, uncolloquial, pulsing with verbal
extravagance. Frost was particularly interested in
imagining the mind and character of a woman who,
typically, as wife or mother or housekeeper, is servant
to others, especially to men. (One of his best poems
in the volume is titled "A Servant to Servants.") He
felt comfortable in allowing his female speakers a
greater range of expression, of "poetry," than he usu-
ally allowed his male ones. Consider the following se-
quence from "The Death of the Hired Man," when
the sympathetic Mary is about to tell her husband that
their hired man, Silas, "has come home to die":

Part of a moon was falling down the west,
Dragging the whole sky with it to the hills.
Its light poured softly in her lap. She saw
And spread her apron to it. She put out her hand
Among the harp-like morning-glory strings,
Taut with the dew from garden bed to eaves,
As if she played unheard the tenderness
That wrought on him beside her in the night.

This "poetical" manner is appropriate to the tremulous moment, rather than—as some critics have thought—a blemish on the poem. In a similarly extravagant manner, the woman in "Home Burial" cries out against her husband's too matter-of-fact acceptance of their infant's death, even to the extent where he had dug the baby's grave with his own hands:

> I saw you from that very window there,
> Making the gravel leap and leap in air,
> Leap up, like that, like that, and land so lightly
> And roll back down the mound beside the hole.

The alliterative repetitions, the consonance and assonance, even the *there/air* rhyme (in a blank verse poem), make this something quite different from common speech. And at the end of "The Black Cottage," the principal speaker, a minister, moves off from his homely reminiscing about the proprietor of the cottage, an old woman he once knew and loved, into a vision of a timeless, changeless state where "truths" could be permanently preserved:

> No one would covet it or think it worth
> The pains of conquering to force change on.
> Scattered oases where men dwelt, but mostly
> Sand dunes held loosely in tamarisk
> Blown over and over themselves in idleness.

From which elevated mood he is jarred back to reality by the sounds of bees in the wall, expressed in a much terser style: "He struck the clapboards, / Fierce heads looked out; small bodies pivoted. / We rose to go. Sunset blazed on the windows."

What has been insufficiently noticed about the poems in *North of Boston*—though Pound called attention to it in his review of the book—is Frost's humor. That humor not only infuses patently comic tall tales like "The Mountain" or "A Hundred Collars" or "The Code," but permeates more "serious" poems like "Mending Wall" and "The Wood-Pile," even showing up at memorable moments in "The Death of the Hired Man" and "The Black Cottage." It is as if to show that, as high as parts of *A Boy's Will* had mounted in lyric apostrophe, so as low into humorous, ironic sense would the poems in *North of Boston* descend. Yet to call the earlier book a book of song, the second one a book of speech, is—as our examples have shown—too simple a distinction. The best poems that triumphantly followed these early volumes—poems like "An Old Man's Winter Night," "To Earthward," "The Most of It," and "Directive"— are both lyric and narrative in their appeal, contain both "high" and "low" levels of diction and style. "I am never more serious than when joking" was one of Frost's claims that is borne out by his poetic career.

That career was temporarily put a halt to by World War I. "Our game is up," he said flatly as he prepared to sail back to America. But he had accomplished more than he imagined he might, if such were possible, and the halt was only temporary. For by the time Frost landed in New York City late in February 1915, what he had once referred to as "the boom" had indeed begun, as editors and critics, then clubs and colleges, began to solicit his poetry and his human presence on podiums and in classrooms. Near the end of his life he mused, "What begins in felicity ends in publicity,"—and, he added, "maybe really *ends* there." It was not, however, in publicity—or not only there— where Frost's career was to end. But it is good to return to these early volumes in which the felicity of his expression is so pure, so satisfyingly and so variously present. They are where the great career began.

—*William H. Pritchard*

A Boy's Will

To
E. M. F.

CONTENTS

PART I

PART II

PART III

PART I

INTO MY OWN

One of my wishes is that those dark trees,
So old and firm they scarcely show the breeze,
Were not, as 'twere, the merest mask of gloom,
But stretched away unto the edge of doom.

I should not be withheld but that some day
Into their vastness I should steal away,
Fearless of ever finding open land,
Or highway where the slow wheel pours the sand.

I do not see why I should e'er turn back,
Or those should not set forth upon my track
To overtake me, who should miss me here
And long to know if still I held them dear.

They would not find me changed from him they knew—
Only more sure of all I thought was true.

GHOST HOUSE

I dwell in a lonely house I know
That vanished many a summer ago,
　And left no trace but the cellar walls,
　And a cellar in which the daylight falls,
And the purple-stemmed wild raspberries grow.

O'er ruined fences the grape-vines shield
The woods come back to the mowing field;
　The orchard tree has grown one copse
　Of new wood and old where the woodpecker chops;
The footpath down to the well is healed.

I dwell with a strangely aching heart
In that vanished abode there far apart
　On that disused and forgotten road
　That has no dust-bath now for the toad.
Night comes; the black bats tumble and dart;

The whippoorwill is coming to shout
And hush and cluck and flutter about:
　I hear him begin far enough away
　Full many a time to say his say
Before he arrives to say it out.

It is under the small, dim, summer star,
I know not who these mute folk are
　Who share the unlit place with me—
　Those stones out under the low-limbed tree
Doubtless bear names that the mosses mar.

They are tireless folk, but slow and sad,
Though two, close-keeping, are lass and lad,—
   With none among them that ever sings,
   And yet, in view of how many things,
As sweet companions as might be had.

MY NOVEMBER GUEST

My Sorrow, when she's here with me,
  Thinks these dark days of autumn rain
Are beautiful as days can be;
She loves the bare, the withered tree;
  She walks the sodden pasture lane.

Her pleasure will not let me stay.
  She talks and I am fain to list:
She's glad the birds are gone away,
She's glad her simple worsted grey
  Is silver now with clinging mist.

The desolate, deserted trees,
  The faded earth, the heavy sky,
The beauties she so truly sees,
She thinks I have no eye for these,
  And vexes me for reason why.

Not yesterday I learned to know
  The love of bare November days
Before the coming of the snow,
But it were vain to tell her so,
  And they are better for her praise.

LOVE AND A QUESTION

A stranger came to the door at eve,
  And he spoke the bridegroom fair.
He bore a green-white stick in his hand,
  And, for all burden, care.
He asked with the eyes more than the lips
  For a shelter for the night,
And he turned and looked at the road afar
  Without a window light.

The bridegroom came forth into the porch
  With "Let us look at the sky,
And question what of the night to be,
  Stranger, you and I."
The woodbine leaves littered the yard,
  The woodbine berries were blue,
Autumn, yes, winter was in the wind;
  "Stranger, I wish I knew."

Within, the bride in the dusk alone
  Bent over the open fire,
Her face rose-red with the glowing coal
  And the thought of the heart's desire.

The bridegroom looked at the weary road,
  Yet saw but her within,
And wished her heart in a case of gold
  And pinned with a silver pin.

The bridegroom thought it little to give
  A dole of bread, a purse,
A heartfelt prayer for the poor of God,
  Or for the rich a curse;

But whether or not a man was asked
   To mar the love of two
By harboring woe in the bridal house,
   The bridegroom wished he knew.

A LATE WALK

When I go up through the mowing field,
  The headless aftermath,
Smooth-laid like thatch with the heavy dew,
  Half closes the garden path.

And when I come to the garden ground,
  The whir of sober birds
Up from the tangle of withered weeds
  Is sadder than any words.

A tree beside the wall stands bare,
  But a leaf that lingered brown,
Disturbed, I doubt not, by my thought,
  Comes softly rattling down.

I end not far from my going forth
  By picking the faded blue
Of the last remaining aster flower
  To carry again to you.

STARS

How countlessly they congregate
  O'er our tumultuous snow,
Which flows in shapes as tall as trees
  When wintry winds do blow!—

As if with keenness for our fate,
  Our faltering few steps on
To white rest, and a place of rest
  Invisible at dawn,—

And yet with neither love nor hate,
  Those stars like some snow-white
Minerva's snow-white marble eyes
  Without the gift of sight.

STORM FEAR

When the wind works against us in the dark,
And pelts with snow
The lower chamber window on the east,
And whispers with a sort of stifled bark,
The beast,
"Come out! Come out!"—
It costs no inward struggle not to go,
Ah, no!
I count our strength,
Two and a child,
Those of us not asleep subdued to mark
How the cold creeps as the fire dies at length,—
How drifts are piled,
Dooryard and road ungraded,
Till even the comforting barn grows far away
And my heart owns a doubt
Whether 'tis in us to arise with day
And save ourselves unaided.

WIND AND WINDOW FLOWER

Lovers, forget your love,
　And list to the love of these,
She a window flower,
　And he a winter breeze.

When the frosty window veil
　Was melted down at noon,
And the cagèd yellow bird
　Hung over her in tune,

He marked her through the pane,
　He could not help but mark,
And only passed her by,
　To come again at dark.

He was a winter wind,
　Concerned with ice and snow,
Dead weeds and unmated birds,
　And little of love could know.

But he sighed upon the sill,
　He gave the sash a shake,
As witness all within
　Who lay that night awake.

Perchance he half prevailed
　To win her for the flight
From the firelit looking-glass
　And warm stove-window light.

But the flower leaned aside
    And thought of naught to say,
And morning found the breeze
    A hundred miles away.

TO THE THAWING WIND

Come with rain, O loud Southwester!
Bring the singer, bring the nester;
Give the buried flower a dream;
Make the settled snow-bank steam;
Find the brown beneath the white;
But whate'er you do to-night,
Bathe my window, make it flow,
Melt it as the ices go;
Melt the glass and leave the sticks
Like a hermit's crucifix;
Burst into my narrow stall;
Swing the picture on the wall;
Run the rattling pages o'er;
Scatter poems on the floor;
Turn the poet out of door.

A PRAYER IN SPRING

Oh, give us pleasure in the flowers to-day;
And give us not to think so far away
As the uncertain harvest; keep us here
And simply in the springing of the year.

Oh, give us pleasure in the orchard white,
Like nothing else by day, like ghosts by night;
And make us happy in the happy bees,
The swarm dilating round the perfect trees.

And make us happy in the darting bird
That suddenly above the bees is heard,
The meteor that thrusts in with needle bill,
And off a blossom in mid air stands still.

For this is love and nothing else is love,
The which it is reserved for God above
To sanctify to what far ends He will,
But which it only needs that we fulfil.

FLOWER-GATHERING

I left you in the morning,
And in the morning glow,
You walked a way beside me
To make me sad to go.
Do you know me in the gloaming,
Gaunt and dusty grey with roaming?
Are you dumb because you know me not,
Or dumb because you know?

All for me? And not a question
For the faded flowers gay
That could take me from beside you
For the ages of a day?
They are yours, and be the measure
Of their worth for you to treasure,
The measure of the little while
That I've been long away.

ROSE POGONIAS

A saturated meadow,
  Sun-shaped and jewel-small,
A circle scarcely wider
  Than the trees around were tall;
Where winds were quite excluded,
  And the air was stifling sweet
With the breath of many flowers,—
  A temple of the heat.

There we bowed us in the burning,
  As the sun's right worship is,
To pick where none could miss them
  A thousand orchises;
For though the grass was scattered,
  Yet every second spear
Seemed tipped with wings of color,
  That tinged the atmosphere.

We raised a simple prayer
  Before we left the spot,
That in the general mowing
  That place might be forgot;
Or if not all so favoured,
  Obtain such grace of hours,
That none should mow the grass there
  While so confused with flowers.

ASKING FOR ROSES

A house that lacks, seemingly, mistress and master,
  With doors that none but the wind ever closes,
Its floor all littered with glass and with plaster;
  It stands in a garden of old-fashioned roses.

I pass by that way in the gloaming with Mary;
  "I wonder," I say, "who the owner of those is."
"Oh, no one you know," she answers me airy,
  "But one we must ask if we want any roses."

So we must join hands in the dew coming coldly
  There in the hush of the wood that reposes,
And turn and go up to the open door boldly,
  And knock to the echoes as beggars for roses.

"Pray, are you within there, Mistress Who-were-you?"
  'Tis Mary that speaks and our errand discloses.
"Pray, are you within there? Bestir you, bestir you!
  'Tis summer again; there's two come for roses.

"A word with you, that of the singer recalling—
  Old Herrick: a saying that every maid knows is
A flower unplucked is but left to the falling,
  And nothing is gained by not gathering roses."

We do not loosen our hands' intertwining
  (Not caring so very much what she supposes),
There when she comes on us mistily shining
  And grants us by silence the boon of her roses.

WAITING

AFIELD AT DUSK

What things for dream there are when spectre-like,
Moving among tall haycocks lightly piled,
I enter alone upon the stubble field,
From which the laborers' voices late have died,
And in the antiphony of afterglow
And rising full moon, sit me down
Upon the full moon's side of the first haycock
And lose myself amid so many alike.

I dream upon the opposing lights of the hour,
Preventing shadow until the moon prevail;
I dream upon the night-hawks peopling heaven,
Each circling each with vague unearthly cry,
Or plunging headlong with fierce twang afar;
And on the bat's mute antics, who would seem
Dimly to have made out my secret place,
Only to lose it when he pirouettes,
And seek it endlessly with purblind haste;

On the last swallow's sweep; and on the rasp
In the abyss of odor and rustle at my back,
That, silenced by my advent, finds once more,
After an interval, his instrument,
And tries once—twice—and thrice if I be there;
And on the worn book of old-golden song
I brought not here to read, it seems, but hold
And freshen in this air of withering sweetness;
But on the memory of one absent most,
For whom these lines when they shall greet her eye.

IN A VALE

When I was young, we dwelt in a vale
  By a misty fen that rang all night,
And thus it was the maidens pale
I knew so well, whose garments trail
  Across the reeds to a window light.

Then fen had every kind of bloom,
  And for every kind there was a face,
And a voice that has sounded in my room
Across the sill from the outer gloom.
  Each came singly unto her place,

But all came every night with the mist;
  And often they brought so much to say
Of things of moment to which, they wist,
One so lonely was fain to list,
  That the stars were almost faded away

Before the last went, heavy with dew,
  Back to the place from which she came—
Where the bird was before it flew,
Where the flower was before it grew,
  Where bird and flower were one and the same.

And thus it is I know so well
  Why the flower has odor, the bird has song.
You have only to ask me, and I can tell.
No, not vainly there did I dwell,
  Nor vainly listen all the night long.

A DREAM PANG

I had withdrawn in forest, and my song
Was swallowed up in leaves that blew away;
And to the forest edge you came one day
(This was my dream) and looked and pondered long,
But did not enter, though the wish was strong:
You shook your pensive head as who should say,
"I dare not—too far in his footsteps stray—
He must seek me would he undo the wrong."

Not far, but near, I stood and saw it all
Behind low boughs the trees let down outside;
And the sweet pang it cost me not to call
And tell you what I saw does still abide.
But 'tis not true that thus I dwelt aloof,
For the wood wakes, and you are here for proof.

IN NEGLECT

They leave us so to the way we took,
  As two in whom they were proved mistaken,
That we sit sometimes in the wayside nook,
With mischievous, vagrant, seraphic look,
  And *try* if we cannot feel forsaken.

THE VANTAGE POINT

If tired of trees I seek again mankind,
 Well I know where to hie me—in the dawn,
 To a slope where the cattle keep the lawn.
There amid lolling juniper reclined,
Myself unseen, I see in white defined
 Far off the homes of men, and farther still,
 The graves of men on an opposing hill,
Living or dead, whichever are to mind.

And if by noon I have too much of these,
 I have but to turn on my arm, and lo,
 The sun-burned hillside sets my face aglow,
My breathing shakes the bluet like a breeze,
 I smell the earth, I smell the bruisèd plant,
 I look into the crater of the ant.

MOWING

There was never a sound beside the wood but one,
And that was my long scythe whispering to the ground.
What was it it whispered? I knew not well myself;
Perhaps it was something about the heat of the sun,
Something, perhaps, about the lack of sound—
And that was why it whispered and did not speak.
It was no dream of the gift of idle hours,
Or easy gold at the hand of fay or elf:
Anything more than the truth would have seemed too
  weak
To the earnest love that laid the swale in rows,
Not without feeble-pointed spikes of flowers
(Pale orchises), and scared a bright green snake.
The fact is the sweetest dream that labor knows.
My long scythe whispered and left the hay to make.

GOING FOR WATER

The well was dry beside the door,
  And so we went with pail and can
Across the fields behind the house
  To seek the brook if still it ran;

Not loth to have excuse to go,
  Because the autumn eve was fair
(Though chill), because the fields were ours,
  And by the brook our woods were there.

We ran as if to meet the moon
  That slowly dawned behind the trees,
The barren boughs without the leaves,
  Without the birds, without the breeze.

But once within the wood, we paused
  Like gnomes that hid us from the moon,
Ready to run to hiding new
  With laughter when she found us soon.

Each laid on the other a staying hand
  To listen ere we dared to look,
And in the hush we joined to make
  We heard, we knew we heard the brook.

A note as from a single place,
  A slender tinkling fall that made
Now drops that floated on the pool
  Like pearls, and now a silver blade.

PART II

REVELATION

We make ourselves a place apart
　　Behind light words that tease and flout,
But oh, the agitated heart
　　Till someone find us really out.

'Tis pity if the case require
　　(Or so we say) that in the end
We speak the literal to inspire
　　The understanding of a friend.

But so with all, from babes that play
　　At hide-and-seek to God afar,
So all who hide too well away
　　Must speak and tell us where they are.

THE TRIAL BY EXISTENCE

Even the bravest that are slain
  Shall not dissemble their surprise
On waking to find valor reign,
  Even as on earth, in paradise;
And where they sought without the sword
  Wide fields of asphodel fore'er,
To find that the utmost reward
  Of daring should be still to dare.

The light of heaven falls whole and white
  And is not shattered into dyes,
The light for ever is morning light;
  The hills are verdured pasture-wise;
The angel hosts with freshness go,
  And seek with laughter what to brave;—
And binding all is the hushed snow
  Of the far-distant breaking wave.

And from a cliff-top is proclaimed
  The gathering of the souls for birth,
The trial by existence named,
  The obscuration upon earth.
And the slant spirits trooping by
  In streams and cross- and counter-streams
Can but give ear to that sweet cry
  For its suggestion of what dreams!

And the more loitering are turned
  To view once more the sacrifice
Of those who for some good discerned
  Will gladly give up paradise.
And a white shimmering concourse rolls

Toward the throne to witness there
The speeding of devoted souls
   Which God makes his especial care.

And none are taken but who will,
   Having first heard the life read out
That opens earthward, good and ill,
   Beyond the shadow of a doubt;
And very beautifully God limns,
   And tenderly, life's little dream,
But naught extenuates or dims,
   Setting the thing that is supreme.

Nor is there wanting in the press
   Some spirit to stand simply forth,
Heroic in its nakedness,
   Against the uttermost of earth.
The tale of earth's unhonored things
   Sounds nobler there than 'neath the sun;
And the mind whirls and the heart sings,
   And a shout greets the daring one.

But always God speaks at the end:
   'One thought in agony of strife
The bravest would have by for friend,
   The memory that he chose the life;
But the pure fate to which you go
   Admits no memory of choice,
Or the woe were not earthly woe
   To which you give the assenting voice.'

And so the choice must be again,
   But the last choice is still the same;
And the awe passes wonder then,
   And a hush falls for all acclaim.
And God has taken a flower of gold
   And broken it, and used therefrom

The mystic link to bind and hold
   Spirit to matter till death come.

'Tis of the essence of life here,
   Though we choose greatly, still to lack
The lasting memory at all clear,
   That life has for us on the wrack
Nothing but what we somehow chose;
   Thus are we wholly stripped of pride
In the pain that has but one close,
   Bearing it crushed and mystified.

IN EQUAL SACRIFICE

Thus of old the Douglas did:
He left his land as he was bid
With the royal heart of Robert the Bruce
In a golden case with a golden lid,

To carry the same to the Holy Land;
By which we can see and understand
That that was the place to carry a heart
At loyalty and love's command,

And that was the case to carry it in.
The Douglas had not far to win
Before he came to the land of Spain,
Where long a holy war had been

Against the too-victorious Moor;
And there his courage could not endure
Not to strike a blow for God
Before he made his errand sure.

And ever it was intended so,
That a man for God should strike a blow,
No matter the heart he has in charge
For the Holy Land where hearts should go.

But when in battle the foe were met,
The Douglas found him sore beset,
With only strength of the fighting arm
For one more battle passage yet—

And that as vain to save the day
As bring his body safe away—

Only a signal deed to do
And a last sounding word to say.

The heart he wore in a golden chain
He swung and flung forth into the plain,
And followed it crying, "Heart or death!"
And fighting over it perished fain.

So may another do of right,
Give a heart to the hopeless fight,
The more of right the more he loves;
So may another redouble might

For a few swift gleams of the angry brand,
Scorning greatly not to demand
In equal sacrifice with his
The heart he bore to the Holy Land.

THE TUFT OF FLOWERS

I went to turn the grass once after one
Who mowed it in the dew before the sun.

The dew was gone that made his blade so keen
Before I came to view the levelled scene.

I looked for him behind an isle of trees;
I listened for his whetstone on the breeze.

But he had gone his way, the grass all mown,
And I must be, as he had been,—alone,

'As all must be,' I said within my heart,
'Whether they work together or apart.'

But as I said it, swift there passed me by
On noiseless wing a 'wildered butterfly,

Seeking with memories grown dim o'er night
Some resting flower of yesterday's delight.

And once I marked his flight go round and round,
As where some flower lay withering on the ground.

And then he flew as far as eye could see,
And then on tremulous wing came back to me.

I thought of questions that have no reply,
And would have turned to toss the grass to dry;

But he turned first, and led my eye to look
At a tall tuft of flowers beside a brook,

A leaping tongue of bloom the scythe had spared
Beside a reedy brook the scythe had bared.

I left my place to know them by their name,
Finding them butterfly weed when I came.

The mower in the dew had loved them thus,
By leaving them to flourish, not for us,

Nor yet to draw one thought of ours to him.
But from sheer morning gladness at the brim.

The butterfly and I had lit upon,
Nevertheless, a message from the dawn,

That made me hear the wakening birds around,
And hear his long scythe whispering to the ground,

And feel a spirit kindred to my own;
So that henceforth I worked no more alone;

But glad with him, I worked as with his aid,
And weary, sought at noon with him the shade;

And dreaming, as it were, held brotherly speech
With one whose thought I had not hoped to reach.

"Men work together," I told him from the heart,
"Whether they work together or apart."

SPOILS OF THE DEAD

Two fairies it was
　On a still summer day
Came forth in the woods
　With the flowers to play.

The flowers they plucked
　They cast on the ground
For others, and those
　For still others they found.

Flower-guided it was
　That they came as they ran
On something that lay
　In the shape of a man.

The snow must have made
　The feathery bed
When this one fell
　On the sleep of the dead.

But the snow was gone
　A long time ago,
And the body he wore
　Nigh gone with the snow.

The fairies drew near
　And keenly espied
A ring on his hand
　And a chain at his side.

They knelt in the leaves
　And eerily played

With the glittering things,
  And were not afraid.

And when they went home
  To hide in their burrow,
They took them along
  To play with to-morrow.

When *you* came on death,
  Did you not come flower-guided
Like the elves in the wood?
  I remember that I did.

But I recognised death
  With sorrow and dread,
And I hated and hate
  The spoils of the dead.

PAN WITH US

Pan came out of the woods one day,—
His skin and his hair and his eyes were grey,
The gray of the moss of walls were they,—
   And stood in the sun and looked his fill
   At wooded valley and wooded hill.

He stood in the zephyr, pipes in hand,
On a height of naked pasture land;
In all the country he did command
   He saw no smoke and he saw no roof.
   That was well! and he stamped a hoof.

His heart knew peace, for none came here
To this lean feeding save once a year
Someone to salt the half-wild steer,
   Or homespun children with clicking pails
   Who see so little they tell no tales.

He tossed his pipes, too hard to teach
A new-world song, far out of reach,
For a sylvan sign that the blue jay's screech
   And the whimper of hawks beside the sun
   Were music enough for him, for one.

Times were changed from what they were:
Such pipes kept less of power to stir
The fruited bough of the juniper
   And the fragile bluets clustered there
   Than the merest aimless breath of air.

They were pipes of pagan mirth,
And the world had found new terms of worth.
He laid him down on the sun-burned earth
   And ravelled a flower and looked away—
   Play? Play?—What should he play?

THE DEMIURGE'S LAUGH

It was far in the sameness of the wood;
  I was running with joy on the Demon's trail,
Though I knew what I hunted was no true god.
  It was just as the light was beginning to fail
That I suddenly heard—all I needed to hear:
It has lasted me many and many a year.

The sound was behind me instead of before,
  A sleepy sound, but mocking half,
As of one who utterly couldn't care.
  The Demon arose from his wallow to laugh,
Brushing the dirt from his eye as he went;
And well I knew what the Demon meant.

I shall not forget how his laugh rang out.
  I felt as a fool to have been so caught,
And checked my steps to make pretence
  It was something among the leaves I sought
(Though doubtful whether he stayed to see).
Thereafter I sat me against a tree.

PART III

NOW CLOSE THE WINDOWS

Now close the windows and hush all the fields;
  If the trees must, let them silently toss;
No bird is singing now, and if there is,
  Be it my loss.

It will be long ere the marshes resume,
  It will be long ere the earliest bird:
So close the windows and not hear the wind,
  But see all wind-stirred.

A LINE-STORM SONG

The line-storm clouds fly tattered and swift,
　　The road is forlorn all day,
Where a myriad snowy quartz stones lift,
　　And the hoof-prints vanish away.
The roadside flowers, too wet for the bee,
　　Expend their bloom in vain.
Come over the hills and far with me,
　　And be my love in the rain.

The birds have less to say for themselves
　　In the wood-world's torn despair
Than now these numberless years the elves,
　　Although they are no less there:
All song of the woods is crushed like some
　　Wild, easily shattered rose.
Come, be my love in the wet woods; come,
　　Where the boughs rain when it blows.

There is the gale to urge behind
　　And bruit our singing down,
And the shallow waters aflutter with wind
　　From which to gather your gown.
What matter if we go clear to the west,
　　And come not through dry-shod?
For wilding brooch shall wet your breast
　　The rain-fresh goldenrod.

Oh, never this whelming east wind swells
　　But it seems like the sea's return
To the ancient lands where it left the shells
　　Before the age of the fern;

And it seems like the time when after doubt
  Our love came back amain.
Oh, come forth into the storm and rout
  And be my love in the rain.

OCTOBER

O hushed October morning mild,
Thy leaves have ripened to the fall;
To-morrow's wind, if it be wild,
Should waste them all.
The crows above the forest call;
To-morrow they may form and go.
O hushed October morning mild,
Begin the hours of this day slow,
Make the day seem to us less brief.
Hearts not averse to being beguiled,
Beguile us in the way you know;
Release one leaf at break of day;
At noon release another leaf;
One from our trees, one far away;
Retard the sun with gentle mist;
Enchant the land with amethyst.
Slow, slow!
For the grapes' sake, if they were all,
Whose leaves already are burnt with frost,
Whose clustered fruit must else be lost—
For the grapes' sake along the wall.

MY BUTTERFLY

Thine emulous fond flowers are dead, too,
And the daft sun-assaulter, he
That frightened thee so oft, is fled or dead:
Save only me
(Nor is it sad to thee!)
Save only me
There is none left to mourn thee in the fields.

The gray grass is not dappled with the snow;
Its two banks have not shut upon the river;
But it is long ago—
It seems forever—
Since first I saw thee glance,
With all the dazzling other ones,
In airy dalliance,
Precipitate in love,
Tossed, tangled, whirled and whirled above,
Like a limp rose-wreath in a fairy dance.

When that was, the soft mist
Of my regret hung not on all the land,
And I was glad for thee,
And glad for me, I wist.

Thou didst not know, who tottered, wandering on
　　high,
That fate had made thee for the pleasure of the wind,
With those great careless wings,
Nor yet did I.

And there were other things:
It seemed God let thee flutter from his gentle clasp:

Then fearful he had let thee win
Too far beyond him to be gathered in,
Snatched thee, o'er eager, with ungentle grasp.

Ah! I remember me
How once conspiracy was rife
Against my life—
The languor of it and the dreaming fond;
Surging, the grasses dizzied me of thought,
The breeze three odors brought,
And a gem-flower waved in a wand!

Then when I was distraught
And could not speak,
Sidelong, full on my cheek,
What should that reckless zephyr fling
But the wild touch of thy dye-dusty wing!

I found that wing broken to-day!
For thou art dead, I said,
And the strange birds say.
I found it with the withered leaves
Under the eaves.

RELUCTANCE

Out through the fields and the woods
  And over the walls I have wended;
I have climbed the hills of view
  And looked at the world, and descended;
I have come by the highway home,
  And lo, it is ended.

The leaves are all dead on the ground,
  Save those that the oak is keeping
To ravel them one by one
  And let them go scraping and creeping
Out over the crusted snow,
  When others are sleeping.

And the dead leaves lie huddled and still,
  No longer blown hither and thither;
The last lone aster is gone;
  The flowers of the witch-hazel wither;
The heart is still aching to seek,
  But the feet question "Whither?"

Ah, when to the heart of man
  Was it ever less than a treason
To go with the drift of things,
  To yield with a grace to reason,
And bow and accept the end
  Of a love or a season?

North of Boston

To
E. M. F.
this book of people

THE PASTURE

I'm going out to clean the pasture spring;
I'll only stop to rake the leaves away
(And wait to watch the water clear, I may):
I sha'n't be gone long.—You come too.

I'm going out to fetch the little calf
That's standing by the mother. It's so young,
It totters when she licks it with her tongue.
I sha'n't be gone long—You come too.

CONTENTS

"Mending Wall" takes up the theme where
"The Tuft of Flowers" in *A Boy's Will*
laid it down.

MENDING WALL

Something there is that doesn't love a wall,
That sends the frozen-ground-swell under it,
And spills the upper boulders in the sun;
And makes gaps even two can pass abreast.
The work of hunters is another thing:
I have come after them and made repair
Where they have left not one stone on a stone,
But they would have the rabbit out of hiding,
To please the yelping dogs. The gaps I mean,
No one has seen them made or heard them made,
But at spring mending-time we find them there.
I let my neighbour know beyond the hill;
And on a day we meet to walk the line
And set the wall between us once again.
We keep the wall between us as we go.
To each the boulders that have fallen to each.
And some are loaves and some so nearly balls
We have to use a spell to make them balance:
"Stay where you are until our backs are turned!"
We wear our fingers rough with handling them.
Oh, just another kind of out-door game.
One on a side. It comes to little more:
There where it is we do not need the wall:
He is all pine and I am apple orchard.
My apple trees will never get across
And eat the cones under his pines, I tell him.
He only says, "Good fences make good neighbours."
Spring is the mischief in me, and I wonder
If I could put a notion in his head:
"*Why* do they make good neighbours? Isn't it
Where there are cows? But here there are no cows.
Before I built a wall I'd ask to know

What I was walling in or walling out,
And to whom I was like to give offence.
Something there is that doesn't love a wall,
That wants it down." I could say, "Elves," to him,
But it's not elves exactly, and I'd rather
He said it for himself. I see him there
Bringing a stone grasped firmly by the top
In each hand, like an old-stone savage armed.
He moves in darkness as it seems to me,
Not of woods only and the shade of trees.
He will not go behind his father's saying,
And he likes having thought of it so well
He says again, "Good fences make good neighbours."

THE DEATH
OF THE HIRED MAN

Mary sat musing on the lamp-flame at the table
Waiting for Warren. When she heard his step,
She ran on tip-toe down the darkened passage
To meet him in the doorway with the news
And put him on his guard. "Silas is back."
She pushed him outward with her through the door
And shut it after her. "Be kind," she said.
She took the market things from Warren's arms
And set them on the porch, then drew him down
To sit beside her on the wooden steps.

"When was I ever anything but kind to him?
But I'll not have the fellow back," he said.
"I told him so last haying, didn't I?
'If he left then,' I said, 'that ended it.'
What good is he? Who else will harbour him
At his age for the little he can do?
What help he is there's no depending on.
Off he goes always when I need him most.
'He thinks he ought to earn a little pay,
Enough at least to buy tobacco with,
So he won't have to beg and be beholden.'
'All right,' I say, 'I can't afford to pay
Any fixed wages, though I wish I could.'
'Someone else can.' 'Then someone else will have to.'
I shouldn't mind his bettering himself
If that was what it was. You can be certain,
When he begins like that, there's someone at him

Trying to coax him off with pocket-money,—
In haying time, when any help is scarce.
In winter he comes back to us. I'm done."

"Sh! not so loud: he'll hear you," Mary said.

"I want him to: he'll have to soon or late."

"He's worn out. He's asleep beside the stove.
When I came up from Rowe's I found him here,
Huddled against the barn-door fast asleep,
A miserable sight, and frightening, too—
You needn't smile—I didn't recognise him—
I wasn't looking for him—and he's changed.
Wait till you see."

        "Where did you say he'd been?"

"He didn't say. I dragged him to the house,
And gave him tea and tried to make him smoke.
I tried to make him talk about his travels.
Nothing would do: he just kept nodding off."

"What did he say? Did he say anything?"

"But little."

        "Anything? Mary, confess
He said he'd come to ditch the meadow for me."

"Warren!"

        "But did he? I just want to know."

"Of course he did. What would you have him say?
Surely you wouldn't grudge the poor old man
Some humble way to save his self-respect.

He added, if you really care to know,
He meant to clear the upper pasture, too.
That sounds like something you have heard before?
Warren, I wish you could have heard the way
He jumbled everything. I stopped to look
Two or three times—he made me feel so queer—
To see if he was talking in his sleep.
He ran on Harold Wilson—you remember—
The boy you had in haying four years since.
He's finished school, and teaching in his college.
Silas declares you'll have to get him back.
He says they two will make a team for work:
Between them they will lay this farm as smooth!
The way he mixed that in with other things.
He thinks young Wilson a likely lad, though daft
On education—you know how they fought
All through July under the blazing sun,
Silas up on the cart to build the load,
Harold along beside to pitch it on.''

"Yes, I took care to keep well out of earshot."

"Well, those days trouble Silas like a dream.
You wouldn't think they would. How some things
    linger!
Harold's young college boy's assurance piqued him.
After so many years he still keeps finding
Good arguments he sees he might have used.
I sympathise. I know just how it feels
To think of the right thing to say too late.
Harold's associated in his mind with Latin.
He asked me what I thought of Harold's saying
He studied Latin like the violin
Because he liked it—that an argument!
He said he couldn't make the boy believe
He could find water with a hazel prong—

Which showed how much good school had ever
    done him.
He wanted to go over that. But most of all
He thinks if he could have another chance
To teach him how to build a load of hay—"

"I know, that's Silas' one accomplishment.
He bundles every forkful in its place,
And tags and numbers it for future reference,
So he can find and easily dislodge it
In the unloading. Silas does that well.
He takes it out in bunches like big birds' nests.
You never see him standing on the hay
He's trying to lift, straining to lift himself."

"He thinks if he could teach him that, he'd be
Some good perhaps to someone in the world.
He hates to see a boy the fool of books.
Poor Silas, so concerned for other folk,
And nothing to look backward to with pride,
And nothing to look forward to with hope,
So now and never any different."

Part of a moon was falling down the west,
Dragging the whole sky with it to the hills.
Its light poured softly in her lap. She saw
And spread her apron to it. She put out her hand
Among the harp-like morning-glory strings,
Taut with the dew from garden bed to eaves,
As if she played unheard the tenderness
That wrought on him beside her in the night.
"Warren," she said, "he has come home to die:
You needn't be afraid he'll leave you this time."

"Home," he mocked gently.

                    "Yes, what else but home?
It all depends on what you mean by home.

Of course he's nothing to us, any more
Than was the hound that came a stranger to us
Out of the woods, worn out upon the trail."

"Home is the place where, when you have to go there,
They have to take you in."

                        "I should have called it
Something you somehow haven't to deserve."

Warren leaned out and took a step or two,
Picked up a little stick, and brought it back
And broke it in his hand and tossed it by.
"Silas has better claim on us you think
Than on his brother? Thirteen little miles
As the road winds would bring him to his door.
Silas has walked that far no doubt to-day.
Why didn't he go there? His brother's rich,
A somebody—director in the bank."

"He never told us that."

                    "We know it though."
"I think his brother ought to help, of course.
I'll see to that if there is need. He ought of right
To take him in, and might be willing to—
He may be better than appearances.
But have some pity on Silas. Do you think
If he'd had any pride in claiming kin
Or anything he looked for from his brother,
He'd keep so still about him all this time?"

"I wonder what's between them."

                          "I can tell you.
Silas is what he is—we wouldn't mind him—
But just the kind that kinsfolk can't abide.

He never did a thing so very bad.
He don't know why he isn't quite as good
As anyone. He won't be made ashamed
To please his brother, worthless though he is."

"*I* can't think Si ever hurt anyone."

"No, but he hurt my heart the way he lay
And rolled his old head on that sharp-edged chair-back.
He wouldn't let me put him on the lounge.
You must go in and see what you can do.
I made the bed up for him there to-night.
You'll be surprised at him—how much he's broken.
His working days are done; I'm sure of it."

"I'd not be in a hurry to say that."

"I haven't been. Go, look, see for yourself.
But, Warren, please remember how it is:
He's come to help you ditch the meadow.
He has a plan. You mustn't laugh at him.
He may not speak of it, and then he may.
I'll sit and see if that small sailing cloud
Will hit or miss the moon."

                       It hit the moon.
Then there were three there, making a dim row,
The moon, the little silver cloud, and she.

Warren returned—too soon, it seemed to her,
Slipped to her side, caught her by her hand and waited.

"Warren," she questioned.

                "Dead," was all he answered.

THE MOUNTAIN

The mountain held the town as in a shadow
I saw so much before I slept there once:
I noticed that I missed stars in the west,
Where its black body cut into the sky.
Near me it seemed: I felt it like a wall
Behind which I was sheltered from a wind.
And yet between the town and it I found,
When I walked forth at dawn to see new things,
Were fields, a river, and beyond, more fields.
The river at the time was fallen away,
And made a widespread brawl on cobble-stones;
But the signs showed what it had done in spring;
Good grass-land gullied out, and in the grass
Ridges of sand, and driftwood stripped of bark.
I crossed the river and swung round the mountain.
And there I met a man who moved so slow
With white-faced oxen in a heavy cart,
It seemed no harm to stop him altogether.

"What town is this?" I asked.

                    "This? Lunenburg."

Then I was wrong: the town of my sojourn,
Beyond the bridge, was not that of the mountain,
But only felt at night its shadowy presence.
"Where is your village? Very far from here?"

"There is no village—only scattered farms.
We were but sixty voters last election.
We can't in nature grow to many more:
That thing takes all the room!" He moved his goad.

The mountain stood there to be pointed at.
Pasture ran up the side a little way,
And then there was a wall of trees with trunks:
After that only tops of trees, and cliffs
Imperfectly concealed among the leaves.
A dry ravine emerged from under boughs
Into the pasture.

                        "That looks like a path.
Is that the way to reach the top from here?—
Not for this morning, but some other time:
I must be getting back to breakfast now."

"I don't advise your trying from this side.
There is no proper path, but those that *have*
Been up, I understand, have climbed from Ladd's.
That's five miles back. You can't mistake the place:
They logged it there last winter some way up.
I'd take you, but I'm bound the other way."

"You've never climbed it?"

                        "I've been on the sides
Deer-hunting and trout-fishing. There's a brook
That starts up on it somewhere—I've heard say
Right on the top, tip-top—a curious thing.
But what would interest you about the brook,
It's always cold in summer, warm in winter.
One of the great sights going is to see
It steam in winter like an ox's breath.
Until the bushes all along its banks
Are inch-deep with the frosty spines and bristles—
You know the kind. Then let the sun shine on it!"

"There ought to be a view around the world
From such a mountain—if it isn't wooded
Clear to the top." I saw through leafy screens

Great granite terraces in sun and shadow,
Shelves one could rest a knee on getting up—
With depths behind him sheer a hundred feet;
Or turn and sit on and look out and down,
With little ferns in crevices at his elbow."

"As to that I can't say. But there's the spring,
Right on the summit, almost like a fountain.
That ought to be worth seeing."

                                    "If it's there.
You never saw it?"

                        "I guess there's no doubt
About its being there. I never saw it.
It may not be right on the very top:
It wouldn't have to be a long way down
To have some head of water from above,
And a *good distance* down might not be noticed
By anyone who'd come a long way up.
One time I asked a fellow climbing it
To look and tell me later how it was."

"What did he say?"

                        "He said there was a lake
Somewhere in Ireland on a mountain top."

"But a lake's different. What about the spring?"

"He never got up high enough to see.
That's why I don't advise your trying this side.
He tried this side. I've always meant to go
And look myself, but you know how it is:
It doesn't seem so much to climb a mountain
You've worked around the foot of all your life.

What would I do? Go in my overalls,
With a big stick, the same as when the cows
Haven't come down to the bars at milking time?
Or with a shotgun for a stray black bear?
'Twouldn't seem real to climb for climbing it."

"I shouldn't climb it if I didn't want to—
Not for the sake of climbing. What's its name?"

"We call it Hor: I don't know if that's right."

"Can one walk around it? Would it be too far?"

"You can drive round and keep in Lunenburg,
But it's as much as ever you can do,
The boundary lines keep in so close to it.
Hor is the township, and the township's Hor—
And a few houses sprinkled round the foot,
Like boulders broken off the upper cliff,
Rolled out a little farther than the rest."

"Warm in December, cold in June, you say?"

"I don't suppose the water's changed at all.
You and I know enough to know it's warm
Compared with cold, and cold compared with warm.
But all the fun's in how you say a thing."

"You've lived here all your life?"

                              "Ever since Hor
Was no bigger than a——" What, I did not hear.
He drew the oxen toward him with light touches
Of his slim goad on nose and offside flank,
Gave them their marching orders and was moving.

A HUNDRED COLLARS

Lancaster bore him—such a little town,
Such a great man. It doesn't see him often
Of late years, though he keeps the old homestead
And sends the children down there with their mother
To run wild in the summer—a little wild.
Sometimes he joins them for a day or two
And sees old friends he somehow can't get near.
They meet him in the general store at night,
Pre-occupied with formidable mail,
Rifling a printed letter as he talks.
They seem afraid. He wouldn't have it so:
Though a great scholar, he's a democrat,
If not at heart, at least on principle.
Lately when coming up to Lancaster
His train being late he missed another train
And had four hours to wait at Woodsville Junction
After eleven o'clock at night. Too tired
To think of sitting such an ordeal out,
He turned to the hotel to find a bed.

"No room," the night clerk said. "Unless——"
Woodsville's a place of shrieks and wandering lamps
And cars that shook and rattle—and *one* hotel.

"You say 'unless.' "

                    "Unless you wouldn't mind
Sharing a room with someone else."

                              "Who is it?"

"A man."

"So I should hope. What kind of man?"

"I know him: he's all right. A man's a man.
Separate beds of course you understand."
The night clerk blinked his eyes and dared him on.

"Who's that man sleeping in the office chair?
Has he had the refusal of my chance?"

"He was afraid of being robbed or murdered.
What do you say?"

     "I'll have to have a bed."

The night clerk led him up three flights of stairs
And down a narrow passage full of doors,
At the last one of which he knocked and entered.
"Lafe, here's a fellow wants to share your room."

"Show him this way. I'm not afraid of him.
I'm not so drunk I can't take care of myself."

The night clerk clapped a bedstead on the foot.
"This will be yours. Good-night," he said, and went.

"Lafe was the name, I think?"

       "Yes, *Lay*fayette.
You got it the first time. And yours?"

         "Magoon.
Doctor Magoon."

   "A Doctor?"

       "Well, a teacher."

"Professor Square-the-circle-till-you're-tired?
Hold on, there's something I don't think of now

That I had on my mind to ask the first
Man that knew anything I happened in with.
I'll ask you later—don't let me forget it."

The Doctor looked at Lafe and looked away.
A man? A brute. Naked above the waist,
He sat there creased and shining in the light,
Fumbling the buttons in a well-starched shirt.
"I'm moving into a size-larger shirt.
I've felt mean lately; mean's no name for it.
I just found what the matter was to-night:
I've been a-choking like a nursery tree
When it outgrows the wire band of its name tag.
I blamed it on the hot spell we've been having.
'Twas nothing but my foolish hanging back,
Not liking to own up I'd grown a size.
Number eighteen this is. What size do you wear?"

The Doctor caught his throat convulsively.
"Oh—ah—fourteen—fourteen."

                              "Fourteen! You say so!
I can remember when I wore fourteen.
And come to think I must have back at home
More than a hundred collars, size fourteen.
Too bad to waste them all. You ought to have them.
They're yours and welcome; let me send them to you.
What makes you stand there on one leg like that?
You're not much further than where Kike left you.
You act as if you wished you hadn't come.
Sit down or lie down, friend; you make me nervous."

The Doctor made a subdued dash for it,
And propped himself at bay against a pillow.

"Not that way, with your shoes on Kike's white bed.
You can't rest that way. Let me pull your shoes off."

"Don't touch me, please—I say, don't touch me, please.
I'll not be put to bed by you, my man."

"Just as you say. Have it your own way then.
'My man' is it? You talk like a professor.
Speaking of who's afraid of who, however,
I'm thinking I have more to lose than you
If anything should happen to be wrong.
Who wants to cut your number fourteen throat!
Let's have a show down as an evidence
Of good faith. There is ninety dollars.
Come, if you're not afraid."

                                   "*I*'m not afraid.
There's five: that's all I carry."

                                   "I can search you?
Where are you moving over to? Stay still.
You'd better tuck your money under you
And sleep on it the way I always do
When I'm with people I don't trust at night."

"Will you believe me if I put it there
Right on the counterpane—that I do trust you?"

"You'd say so, Mister Man.—I'm a collector.
My ninety isn't mine—you won't think that.
I pick it up a dollar at a time
All round the country for the *Weekly News,*
Published in Bow. You know the *Weekly News*?"

"Known it since I was young."

                                   "Then you know me.
Now we are getting on together—talking.
I'm sort of Something for it at the front.
My business is to find what people want:

They pay for it, and so they ought to have it.
Fairbanks, he says to me—he's editor—
Feel out the public sentiment—he says.
A good deal comes on me when all is said.
The only trouble is we disagree
In politics: I'm Vermont Democrat—
You know what that is, sort of double-dyed;
The *News* has always been Republican.
Fairbanks, he says to me, 'Help us this year,'
Meaning by us their ticket. 'No,' I says,
'I can't and won't. You've been in long enough:
It's time you turned around and boosted us.
You'll have to pay me more than ten a week
If I'm expected to elect Bill Taft.
I doubt if I could do it anyway.' "

"You seem to shape the paper's policy."

"You see I'm in with everybody, know 'em all.
I almost know their farms as well as they do."

"You drive around? It must be pleasant work."

"It's business, but I can't say it's not fun.
What I like best's the lay of different farms,
Coming out on them from a stretch of woods,
Or over a hill or round a sudden corner.
I like to find folks getting out in spring,
Raking the dooryard, working near the house.
Later they get out further in the fields.
Everything's shut sometimes except the barn;
The family's all away in some back meadow.
There's a hay load a-coming—when it comes.
And later still they all get driven in:
The fields are stripped to lawn, the garden patches
Stripped to bare ground, the apple trees
To whips and poles. There's nobody about.

The chimney, though, keeps up a good brisk smoking.
And I lie back and ride. I take the reins
Only when someone's coming, and the mare
Stops when she likes: I tell her when to go.
I've spoiled Jemima in more ways than one.
She's got so she turns in at every house
As if she had some sort of curvature,
No matter if I have no errand there.
She thinks I'm sociable. I maybe am.
It's seldom I get down except for meals, though.
Folks entertain me from the kitchen doorstep,
All in a family row down to the youngest."

"One would suppose they might not be as glad
To see you as you are to see them."

                      "Oh,
Because I want their dollar. I don't want
Anything they've not got. I never dun.
I'm there, and they can pay me if they like.
I go nowhere on purpose: I happen by.
Sorry there is no cup to give you a drink.
I drink out of the bottle—not your style.
Mayn't I offer you——?"

                    "No, no, no, thank you."

"Just as you say. Here's looking at you then.—
And now I'm leaving you a little while.
You'll rest easier when I'm gone, perhaps—
Lie down—let yourself go and get some sleep.
But first—let's see—what was I going to ask you?
Those collars—who shall I address them to,
Suppose you aren't awake when I come back?"

"Really, friend, I can't let you. You—may need them."

"Not till I shrink, when they'll be out of style."

"But really I—I have so many collars."

"I don't know who I rather would have have them.
They're only turning yellow where they are.
But you're the doctor as the saying is.
I'll put the light out. Don't you wait for me:
I've just begun the night. You get some sleep.
I'll knock so-fashion and peep round the door
When I come back so you'll know who it is.
There's nothing I'm afraid of like scared people.
I don't want you should shoot me in the head.
What am I doing carrying off this bottle?
There now, you get some sleep."

He shut the door.
The Doctor slid a little down the pillow.

HOME BURIAL

He saw her from the bottom of the stairs
Before she saw him. She was starting down,
Looking back over her shoulder at some fear.
She took a doubtful step and then undid it
To raise herself and look again. He spoke
Advancing toward her: "What is it you see
From up there always—for I want to know."
She turned and sank upon her skirts at that,
And her face changed from terrified to dull.
He said to gain time: "What is it you see,"
Mounting until she cowered under him.
"I will find out now—you must tell me, dear."
She, in her place, refused him any help
With the least stiffening of her neck and silence.
She let him look, sure that he wouldn't see,
Blind creature; and a while he didn't see.
But at last he murmured, "Oh," and again, "Oh."

"What is it—what?" she said.

                                   "Just that I see."

"You don't," she challenged. "Tell me what it is."

"The wonder is I didn't see at once.
I never noticed it from here before.
I must be wonted to it—that's the reason.
The little graveyard where my people are!
So small the window frames the whole of it.
Not so much larger than a bedroom, is it?
There are three stones of slate and one of marble,

Broad-shouldered little slabs there in the sunlight
On the sidehill. We haven't to mind *those*.
But I understand: it is not the stones,
But the child's mound——"

       "Don't, don't, don't, don't," she cried.

She withdrew shrinking from beneath his arm
That rested on the banister, and slid downstairs;
And turned on him with such a daunting look,
He said twice over before he knew himself:
"Can't a man speak of his own child he's lost?"

"Not you! Oh, where's my hat? Oh, I don't need it!
I must get out of here. I must get air.
I don't know rightly whether any man can."

"Amy! Don't go to someone else this time.
Listen to me. I won't come down the stairs."
He sat and fixed his chin between his fists.
"There's something I should like to ask you, dear."

"You don't know how to ask it."

       "Help me, then."
Her fingers moved the latch for all reply.

"My words are nearly always an offence.
I don't know how to speak of anything
So as to please you. But I might be taught
I should suppose. I can't say I see how.
A man must partly give up being a man
With women-folk. We could have some arrangement
By which I'd bind myself to keep hands off
Anything special you're a-mind to name.
Though I don't like such things 'twixt those that love.
Two that don't love can't live together without them.

But two that do can't live together with them."
She moved the latch a little. "Don't—don't go.
Don't carry it to someone else this time.
Tell me about it if it's something human.
Let me into your grief. I'm not so much
Unlike other folks as your standing there
Apart would make me out. Give me my chance.
I do think, though, you overdo it a little.
What was it brought you up to think it the thing
To take your mother-loss of a first child
So inconsolably—in the face of love.
You'd think his memory might be satisfied——"

"There you go sneering now!"

                              "I'm not, I'm not!
You make me angry. I'll come down to you.
God, what a woman! And it's come to this,
A man can't speak of his own child that's dead."

"You can't because you don't know how.
If you had any feelings, you that dug
With your own hand—how could you?—his little
   grave;
I saw you from that very window there,
Making the gravel leap and leap in air,
Leap up, like that, like that, and land so lightly
And roll back down the mound beside the hole.
I thought, Who is that man? I didn't know you.
And I crept down the stairs and up the stairs
To look again, and still your spade kept lifting.
Then you came in. I heard your rumbling voice
Out in the kitchen, and I don't know why,
But I went near to see with my own eyes.
You could sit there with the stains on your shoes
Of the fresh earth from your own baby's grave
And talk about your everyday concerns.

You had stood the spade up against the wall
Outside there in the entry, for I saw it."

"I shall laugh the worst laugh I ever laughed.
I'm cursed. God, if I don't believe I'm cursed."

"I can repeat the very words you were saying.
'Three foggy mornings and one rainy day
Will rot the best birch fence a man can build.'
Think of it, talk like that at such a time!
What had how long it takes a birch to rot
To do with what was in the darkened parlour.
You *couldn't* care! The nearest friends can go
With anyone to death, comes so far short
They might as well not try to go at all.
No, from the time when one is sick to death,
One is alone, and he dies more alone.
Friends make pretence of following to the grave,
But before one is in it, their minds are turned
And making the best of their way back to life
And living people, and things they understand.
But the world's evil. I won't have grief so
If I can change it. Oh, I won't, I won't!"

"There, you have said it all and you feel better.
You won't go now. You're crying. Close the door.
The heart's gone out of it: why keep it up.
Amy! There's someone coming down the road!"

"*You*—oh, you think the talk is all. I must go—
Somewhere out of this house. How can I make you——"

"If—you—do!" She was opening the door wider.
"Where do you mean to go? First tell me that.
I'll follow and bring you back by force. I *will!*—"

THE BLACK COTTAGE

We chanced in passing by that afternoon
To catch it in a sort of special picture
Among tar-banded ancient cherry trees,
Set well back from the road in rank lodged grass,
The little cottage we were speaking of,
A front with just a door between two windows,
Fresh painted by the shower a velvet black.
We paused, the minister and I, to look.
He made as if to hold it at arm's length
Or put the leaves aside that framed it in.
"Pretty," he said. "Come in. No one will care."
The path was a vague parting in the grass
That led us to a weathered window-sill.
We pressed our faces to the pane. "You see," he said,
"Everything's as she left it when she died.
Her sons won't sell the house or the things in it.
They say they mean to come and summer here
Where they were boys. They haven't come this year.
They live so far away—one is out west—
It will be hard for them to keep their word.
Anyway they won't have the place disturbed."
A buttoned hair-cloth lounge spread scrolling arms
Under a crayon portrait on the wall
Done sadly from an old daguerreotype.
"That was the father as he went to war.
She always, when she talked about war,
Sooner or later came and leaned, half knelt
Against the lounge beside it, though I doubt
If such unlifelike lines kept power to stir
Anything in her after all these years.
He fell at Gettysburg or Fredericksburg,
I ought to know—it makes a difference which:

Fredericksburg wasn't Gettysburg, of course.
But what I'm getting to is how forsaken
A little cottage this has always seemed;
Since she went more than ever, but before—
I don't mean altogether by the lives
That had gone out of it, the father first,
Then the two sons, till she was left alone.
(Nothing could draw her after those two sons.
She valued the considerate neglect
She had at some cost taught them after years.)
I mean by the world's having passed it by—
As we almost got by this afternoon.
It always seems to me a sort of mark
To measure how far fifty years have brought us.
Why not sit down if you are in no haste?
These doorsteps seldom have a visitor.
The warping boards pull out their own old nails
With none to tread and put them in their place.
She had her own idea of things, the old lady.
And she liked talk. She had seen Garrison
And Whittier, and had her story of them.
One wasn't long in learning that she thought
Whatever else the Civil War was for
It wasn't just to keep the States together,
Nor just to free the slaves, though it did both.
She wouldn't have believed those ends enough
To have given outright for them all she gave.
Her giving somehow touched the principle
That all men are created free and equal.
And to hear her quaint phrases—so removed
From the world's view to-day of all those things.
That's a hard mystery of Jefferson's.
What did he mean? Of course the easy way
Is to decide it simply isn't true.
It may not be. I heard a fellow say so.
But never mind, the Welshman got it planted
Where it will trouble us a thousand years.

Each age will have to reconsider it.
You couldn't tell her what the West was saying,
And what the South to her serene belief.
She had some art of hearing and yet not
Hearing the latter wisdom of the world.
White was the only race she ever knew.
Black she had scarcely seen, and yellow never.
But how could they be made so very unlike
By the same hand working in the same stuff?
She had supposed the war decided that.
What are you going to do with such a person?
Strange how such innocence gets its own way.
I shouldn't be surprised if in this world
It were the force that would at last prevail.
Do you know but for her there was a time
When to please younger members of the church,
Or rather say non-members in the church,
Whom we all have to think of nowadays,
I would have changed the Creed a very little?
Not that she ever had to ask me not to;
It never got so far as that; but the bare thought
Of her old tremulous bonnet in the pew,
And of her half asleep was too much for me.
Why, I might wake her up and startle her.
It was the words 'descended into Hades'
That seemed too pagan to our liberal youth.
You know they suffered from a general onslaught.
And well, if they weren't true why keep right on
Saying them like the heathen? We could drop them.
Only—there was the bonnet in the pew.
Such a phrase couldn't have meant much to her.
But suppose she had missed it from the Creed.
As a child misses the unsaid Good-night,
And falls asleep with heartache—how should *I* feel?
I'm just as glad she made me keep hands off,
For, dear me, why abandon a belief
Merely because it ceases to be true.

Cling to it long enough, and not a doubt
It will turn true again, for so it goes.
Most of the change we think we see in life
Is due to truths being in and out of favour.
As I sit here, and oftentimes, I wish
I could be monarch of a desert land
I could devote and dedicate forever
To the truths we keep coming back and back to.
So desert it would have to be, so walled
By mountain ranges half in summer snow,
No one would covet it or think it worth
The pains of conquering to force change on.
Scattered oases where men dwelt, but mostly
Sand dunes held loosely in tamarisk
Blown over and over themselves in idleness.
Sand grains should sugar in the natal dew
The babe born to the desert, the sand storm
Retard mid-waste my cowering caravans—

"There are bees in this wall." He struck the clapboards,
Fierce heads looked out; small bodies pivoted.
We rose to go. Sunset blazed on the windows.

BLUEBERRIES

"You ought to have seen what I saw on my way
To the village, through Mortenson's pasture to-day:
Blueberries as big as the end of your thumb,
Real sky-blue, and heavy, and ready to drum
In the cavernous pail of the first one to come!
And all ripe together, not some of them green
And some of them ripe! You ought to have seen!"

"I don't know what part of the pasture you mean."

"You know where they cut off the woods—let me see—
It was two years ago—or no!—can it be
No longer than that?—and the following fall
The fire ran and burned it all up but the wall."

"Why, there hasn't been time for the bushes to grow.
That's always the way with the blueberries, though:
There may not have been the ghost of a sign
Of them anywhere under the shade of the pine,
But get the pine out of the way, you may burn
The pasture all over until not a fern
Or grass-blade is left, not to mention a stick,
And presto, they're up all around you as thick
And hard to explain as a conjuror's trick."

"It must be on charcoal they fatten their fruit.
I taste in them sometimes the flavour of soot.
And after all really they're ebony skinned:
The blue's but a mist from the breath of the wind,
A tarnish that goes at a touch of the hand,
And less than the tan with which pickers are tanned."

"Does Mortenson know what he has, do you think?"

"He may and not care and so leave the chewink
To gather them for him—you know what he is.
He won't make the fact that they're rightfully his
An excuse for keeping us other folk out."

"I wonder you didn't see Loren about."

"The best of it was that I did. Do you know,
I was just getting through what the field had to show
And over the wall and into the road,
When who should come by, with a democrat-load
Of all the young chattering Lorens alive,
But Loren, the fatherly, out for a drive."

"He saw you, then? What did he do? Did he frown?"

"He just kept nodding his head up and down.
You know how politely he always goes by.
But he thought a big thought—I could tell by his
eye—
Which being expressed, might be this in effect:
'I have left those there berries, I shrewdly suspect,
To ripen too long. I am greatly to blame.'"

"He's a thriftier person than some I could name."

"He seems to be thrifty; and hasn't he need,
With the mouths of all those young Lorens to feed?
He has brought them all up on wild berries, they say,
Like birds. They store a great many away.
They eat them the year round, and those they don't eat
They sell in the store and buy shoes for their feet."

"Who cares what they say? It's a nice way to live,
Just taking what Nature is willing to give,
Not forcing her hand with harrow and plow."

"I wish you had seen his perpetual bow—
And the air of the youngsters! Not one of them
   turned,
And they looked so solemn-absurdly concerned."

"I wish I knew half what the flock of them know
Of where all the berries and other things grow,
Cranberries in bogs and raspberries on top
Of the boulder-strewn mountain, and when they will
   crop.
I met them one day and each had a flower
Stuck into his berries as fresh as a shower;
Some strange kind—they told me it hadn't a name."

"I've told you how once not long after we came,
I almost provoked poor Loren to mirth
By going to him of all people on earth
To ask if he knew any fruit to be had
For the picking. The rascal, he said he'd be glad
To tell if he knew. But the year had been bad.
There *had* been some berries—but those were all
   gone.
He didn't say where they had been. He went on:
'I'm sure—I'm sure'—as polite as could be.
He spoke to his wife in the door, 'Let me see,
Mame, *we* don't know any good berrying place?'
It was all he could do to keep a straight face."

"If he thinks all the fruit that grows wild is for him,
He'll find he's mistaken. See here, for a whim,
We'll pick in the Mortensons' pasture this year.
We'll go in the morning, that is, if it's clear,
And the sun shines out warm: the vines must be wet.
It's so long since I picked I almost forget
How we used to pick berries: we took one look round,
Then sank out of sight like trolls underground,
And saw nothing more of each other, or heard,

Unless when you said I was keeping a bird
Away from its nest, and I said it was you.
'Well, one of us is.' For complaining it flew
Around and around us. And then for a while
We picked, till I feared you had wandered a mile,
And I thought I had lost you. I lifted a shout
Too loud for the distance you were, it turned out,
For when you made answer, your voice was as low
As talking—you stood up beside me, you know."

"We sha'n't have the place to ourselves to enjoy—
Not likely, when all the young Lorens deploy.
They'll be there to-morrow, or even to-night.
They won't be too friendly—they may be polite—
To people they look on as having no right
To pick where they're picking. But we won't complain.
You ought to have seen how it looked in the rain,
The fruit mixed with water in layers of leaves,
Like two kinds of jewels, a vision for thieves."

A SERVANT TO SERVANTS

I didn't make you know how glad I was
To have you come and camp here on our land.
I promised myself to get down some day
And see the way you lived, but I don't know!
With a houseful of hungry men to feed
I guess you'd find. . . . It seems to me
I can't express my feelings any more
Than I can raise my voice or want to lift
My hand (oh, I can lift it when I have to).
Did ever you feel so? I hope you never.
It's got so I don't even know for sure
Whether I *am* glad, sorry, or anything.
There's nothing but a voice-like left inside
That seems to tell me how I ought to feel,
And would feel if I wasn't all gone wrong.
You take the lake. I look and look at it.
I see it's a fair, pretty sheet of water.
I stand and make myself repeat out loud
The advantages it has, so long and narrow,
Like a deep piece of some running river
Cut short off at both ends. It lies five miles
Straight away through the mountain notch
From the sink window where I wash the plates,
And all our storms come up toward the house,
Drawing the slow waves whiter and whiter and whiter.
It took my mind off doughnuts and soda biscuit
To step outdoors and take the water dazzle
A sunny morning, or take the rising wind
About my face and body and through my wrapper,
When a storm threatened from the Dragon's Den,
And a cold chill shivered across the lake.
I see it's a fair, pretty sheet of water,

Our Willoughby! How did you hear of it?
I expect, though, everyone's heard of it.
In a book about ferns? Listen to that!
You let things more like feathers regulate
Your going and coming. And you like it here?
I can see how you might. But I don't know!
It would be different if more people came,
For then there would be business. As it is,
The cottages Len built, sometimes we rent them,
Sometime we don't. We've a good piece of shore
That ought to be worth something, and may yet.
But I don't count on it as much as Len.
He looks on the bright side of everything,
Including me. He thinks I'll be all right
With doctoring. But it's not medicine—
Lowe is the only doctor's dared to say so—
It's rest I want—there, I have said it out—
From cooking meals for hungry hired men
And washing dishes after them—from doing
Things over and over that just won't stay done.
By good rights I ought not to have so much
Put on me, but there seems no other way.
Len says one steady pull more ought to do it.
Len says the best way out is always through.
And I agree to that, or in so far
As that I can see no way out but through—
Leastways for me—and then they'll be convinced.
It's not that Len don't want the best for me.
It was his plan our moving over in
Beside the lake from where that day I showed you
We used to live—ten miles from anywhere.
We didn't change without some sacrifice,
But Len went at it to make up the loss.
His work's a man's, of course, from sun to sun,
But he works when he works as hard as I do—
Though there's small profit in comparisons.
(Women and men will make them all the same.)

But work ain't all. Len undertakes too much.
He's into everything in town. This year
It's highways, and he's got too many men
Around him to look after that make waste.
They take advantage of him shamefully,
And proud, too, of themselves for doing so.
We have four here to board, great good-for-nothings,
Sprawling about the kitchen with their talk
While I fry their bacon. Much they care!
No more put out in what they do or say
Than if I wasn't in the room at all.
Coming and going all the time, they are:
I don't learn what their names are, let alone
Their characters, or whether they are safe
To have inside the house with doors unlocked.
I'm not afraid of them, though, if they're not
Afraid of me. There's two can play at that.
I have my fancies: it runs in the family.
My father's brother wasn't right. They kept him
Locked up for years back there at the old farm.
I've been away once—yes, I've been away.
The State Asylum. I was prejudiced;
I wouldn't have sent anyone of mine there;
You know the old idea—the only asylum
Was the poorhouse, and those who could afford,
Rather than send their folks to such a place,
Kept them at home; and it does seem more human.
But it's not so: the place is the asylum.
There they have every means proper to do with,
And you aren't darkening other people's lives—
Worse than no good to them, and they no good
To you in your condition; you can't know
Affection or the want of it in that state.
I've heard too much of the old-fashioned way.
My father's brother, he went mad quite young.
Some thought he had been bitten by a dog,
Because his violence took on the form

Of carrying about his pillow in his teeth;
But it's more likely he was crossed in love,
Or so the story goes. It was some girl.
Anyway all he talked about was love.
They soon saw he would do someone a mischief
If he wa'n't kept strict watch of, and it ended
In father's building him a sort of cage,
Or room within a room, of hickory poles,
Like stanchions in the barn, from floor to ceiling,—
A narrow passage all the way around.
Anything they put in for furniture
He'd tear to pieces, even a bed to lie on.
So they made the place comfortable with straw,
Like a beast's stall, to ease their consciences.
Of course they had to feed him without dishes.
They tried to keep him clothed, but he paraded
With his clothes on his arm—all of his clothes.
Cruel—it sounds. I 'spose they did the best
They knew. And just when he was at the height,
Father and mother married, and mother came,
A bride, to help take care of such a creature,
And accommodate her young life to his.
That was what marrying father meant to her.
She had to lie and hear love things made dreadful
By his shouts in the night. He'd shout and shout
Until the strength was shouted out of him,
And his voice died down slowly from exhaustion.
He'd pull the bars apart like bow and bow-string,
And let them go and make them twang until
His hands had worn them smooth as any ox-bow.
And then he'd crow as if he thought that child's play—
The only fun he had. I've heard them say, though,
They found a way to put a stop to it.
He was before my time—I never saw him;
But the pen stayed exactly as it was
There in the upper chamber in the ell,
A sort of catch-all full of attic clutter.

I often think of the smooth hickory bars.
It got so I would say—you know, half fooling—
"It's time I took my turn upstairs in jail"—
Just as you will till it becomes a habit.
No wonder I was glad to get away.
Mind you, I waited till Len said the word.
I didn't want the blame if things went wrong.
I was glad though, no end, when we moved out,
And I looked to be happy, and I was,
As I said, for a while—but I don't know!
Somehow the change wore out like a prescription.
And there's more to it than just window-views
And living by a lake. I'm past such help—
Unless Len took the notion, which he won't,
And I won't ask him—it's not sure enough.
I 'spose I've got to go the road I'm going:
Other folks have to, and why shouldn't I?
I almost think if I could do like you,
Drop everything and live out on the ground—
But it might be, come night, I shouldn't like it,
Or a long rain. I should soon get enough,
And be glad of a good roof overhead.
I've lain awake thinking of you, I'll warrant,
More than you have yourself, some of these nights.
The wonder was the tents weren't snatched away
From over you as you lay in your beds.
I haven't courage for a risk like that.
Bless you, of course, you're keeping me from work,
But the thing of it is, I need to *be* kept.
There's work enough to do—there's always that;
But behind's behind. The worst that you can do
Is set me back a little more behind.
I sha'n't catch up in this world, anyway.
I'd *rather* you'd not go unless you must.

AFTER APPLE-PICKING

My long two-pointed ladder's sticking through a tree
Toward heaven still,
And there's a barrel that I didn't fill
Beside it, and there may be two or three
Apples I didn't pick upon some bough.
But I am done with apple-picking now.
Essence of winter sleep is on the night,
The scent of apples: I am drowsing off.
I cannot rub the strangeness from my sight
I got from looking through a pane of glass
I skimmed this morning from the drinking trough
And held against the world of hoary grass.
It melted, and I let it fall and break.
But I was well
Upon my way to sleep before it fell,
And I could tell
What form my dreaming was about to take.
Magnified apples appear and disappear,
Stem end and blossom end,
And every fleck of russet showing clear.
My instep arch not only keeps the ache,
It keeps the pressure of a ladder-round.
I feel the ladder sway as the boughs bend.
And I keep hearing from the cellar bin
The rumbling sound
Of load on load of apples coming in.
For I have had too much
Of apple-picking: I am overtired
Of the great harvest I myself desired.
There were ten thousand thousand fruit to touch,
Cherish in hand, lift down, and not let fall.

For all
That struck the earth,
No matter if not bruised or spiked with stubble,
Went surely to the cider-apple heap
As of no worth.
One can see what will trouble
This sleep of mine, whatever sleep it is.
Were he not gone,
The woodchuck could say whether it's like his
Long sleep, as I describe its coming on,
Or just some human sleep.

THE CODE

There were three in the meadow by the brook
Gathering up windrows, piling cocks of hay,
With an eye always lifted toward the west
Where an irregular sun-bordered cloud
Darkly advanced with a perpetual dagger
Flickering across its bosom. Suddenly
One helper, thrusting pitchfork in the ground,
Marched himself off the field and home. One stayed.
The town-bred farmer failed to understand.

"What is there wrong?"

                    "Something you just now said."

"What did I say?"

                    "About our taking pains."

"To cock the hay?—because it's going to shower?
I said that more than half an hour ago.
I said it to myself as much as you."

"You didn't know. But James is one big fool.
He thought you meant to find fault with his work.
That's what the average farmer would have meant.
James would take time, of course, to chew it over
Before he acted: he'd just got round to act."

"He is a fool if that's the way he takes me."

"Don't let it bother you. You've found out something.
The hand that knows his business won't be told

To do work better or faster—those two things.
I'm as particular as anyone:
Most likely I'd have served you just the same.
But I know you don't understand our ways.
You were just talking what was in your mind,
What was in all our minds, and you weren't hinting.
Tell you a story of what happened once:
I was up here in Salem at a man's
Named Sanders with a gang of four or five
Doing the haying. No one liked the boss.
He was one of the kind sports call a spider,
All wiry arms and legs that spread out wavy
From a humped body nigh as big's a biscuit.
But work! that man could work, especially
If by so doing he could get more work
Out of his hired help. I'm not denying
He was hard on himself. I couldn't find
That he kept any hours—not for himself.
Daylight and lantern-light were one to him:
I've heard him pounding in the barn all night.
But what he liked was someone to encourage.
Them that he couldn't lead he'd get behind
And drive, the way you can, you know, in mowing—
Keep at their heels and threaten to mow their legs off.
I'd seen about enough of his bulling tricks
(We call that bulling). I'd been watching him.
So when he paired off with me in the hayfield
To load the load, thinks I, Look out for trouble.
I built the load and topped it off; old Sanders
Combed it down with a rake and says, 'O.K.'
Everything went well till we reached the barn
With a big catch to empty in a bay.
You understand that meant the easy job
For the man up on top of throwing *down*
The hay and rolling it off wholesale,
Where on a mow it would have been slow lifting.
You wouldn't think a fellow'd need much urging

Under these circumstances, would you now?
But the old fool seizes his fork in both hands,
And looking up bewhiskered out of the pit,
Shouts like an army captain, 'Let her come!'
Thinks I, D'ye meant it? 'What was that you said?'
I asked out loud, so's there'd be no mistake,
'Did you say, Let her come?' 'Yes, let her come.'
He said it over, but he said it softer.
Never you say a thing like that to a man,
Not if he values what he is. God, I'd as soon
Murdered him as left out his middle name.
I'd built the load and knew right where to find it.
Two or three forkfuls I picked lightly round for
Like meditating, and then I just dug in
And dumped the rackful on him in ten lots.
I looked over the side once in the dust
And caught sight of him treading-water-like,
Keeping his head above. 'Damn ye,' I says,
'That gets ye!' He squeaked like a squeezed rat.
That was the last I saw or heard of him.
I cleaned the rack and drove out to cool off.
As I sat mopping hayseed from my neck,
And sort of waiting to be asked about it,
One of the boys sings out, 'Where's the old man?'
'I left him in the barn under the hay.
If ye want him, ye can go and dig him out.'
They realized from the way I swobbed my neck
More than was needed something must be up.
They headed for the barn; I stayed where I was.
They told me afterward. First they forked hay,
A lot of it, out into the barn floor.
Nothing! Then they listened for him. Not a rustle.
I guess they thought I'd spiked him in the temple
Before I buried him, or I couldn't have managed.
They excavated more. 'Go keep his wife
Out of the barn.' Someone looked in a window,
And curse me if he wasn't in the kitchen

Slumped way down in a chair, with both his feet
Stuck in the oven, the hottest day that summer.
He looked so clean disgusted from behind
There was no one that dared to stir him up,
Or let him know that he was being looked at.
Apparently I hadn't buried him
(I may have knocked him down); but my just trying
To bury him had hurt his dignity.
He had gone to the house so's not to meet me.
He kept away from us all afternoon.
We tended to his hay. We saw him out
After a while picking peas in his garden:
He couldn't keep away from doing something."

"Weren't you relieved to find he wasn't dead?"

"No! and yet I don't know—it's hard to say.
I went about to kill him fair enough."

"You took an awkward way. Did he discharge you?"

"Discharge me? No! He knew I did just right."

THE GENERATIONS OF MEN

A governor it was proclaimed this time,
When all who would come seeking in New Hampshire
Ancestral memories might come together.
And those of the name Stark gathered in Bow,
A rock-strewn town where farming has fallen off,
And sprout-lands flourish where the axe has gone.
Someone had literally run to earth
In an old cellar hole in a by-road
The origin of all the family there.
Thence they were sprung, so numerous a tribe
That now not all the houses left in town
Made shift to shelter them without the help
Of here and there a tent in grove and orchard.
They were at Bow, but that was not enough:
Nothing would do but they must fix a day
To stand together on the crater's verge
That turned them on the world, and try to fathom
The past and get some strangeness out of it.
But rain spoiled all. The day began uncertain,
With clouds low trailing and moments of rain that
    misted.
The young folk held some hope out to each other
Till well toward noon when the storm settled down
With a swish in the grass. "What if the others
Are there," they said. "It isn't going to rain."
Only one from a farm not far away
Strolled thither, not expecting he would find
Anyone else, but out of idleness.
One, and one other, yes, for there were two.
The second round the curving hillside road
Was a girl; and she halted some way off
To reconnoitre, and then make up her mind

At least to pass by and see who he was,
And perhaps hear some word about the weather.
This was some Stark she didn't know. He nodded.
"No fête to-day," he said.

                              "It looks that way."

She swept the heavens, turning on her heel.
"I only idled down."

          "I idled down."

Provision there had been for just such meeting
Of stranger cousins, in a family tree
Drawn on a sort of passport with the branch
Of the one bearing it done in detail—
Some zealous one's laborious device.
She made a sudden movement toward her bodice,
As one who clasps her heart. They laughed together.
"Stark?" he inquired. "No matter for the proof."

"Yes, Stark. And you?"

                    "I'm Stark." He drew his passport.

"You know we might not be and still be cousins:
The town is full of Chases, Lowes, and Baileys,
All claiming some priority in Starkness.
My mother was a Lane, yet might have married
Anyone upon earth and still her children
Would have been Starks, and doubtless here to-day."

"You riddle with your genealogy
Like a Viola. I don't follow you."

"I only mean my mother was a Stark
Several times over, and by marrying father
No more than brought us back into the name."

"One ought not to be thrown into confusion
By a plain statement of relationship,
But I own what you say makes my head spin.
You take my card—you seem so good at such things—
And see if you can reckon our cousinship.
Why not take seats here on the cellar wall
And dangle feet among the raspberry vines?"

"Under the shelter of the family tree."

"Just so—that ought to be enough protection."

"Not from the rain. I think it's going to rain."

"It's raining."

                "No, it's misting: let's be fair.
Does the rain seem to you to cool the eyes?"

The situation was like this: the road
Bowed outward on the mountain half-way up,
And disappeared and ended not far off.
No one went home that way. The only house
Beyond where they were was a shattered seed-pod.
And below roared a brook hidden in trees,
The sound of which was silence for the place.
This he sat listening to till she gave judgment.

"On father's side, it seems, we're—let me see——"

"Don't be too technical.—You have three cards."

"Four cards, one yours, three mine, one for each branch
Of the Stark family I'm a member of."

"D'you know a person so related to herself

Is supposed to be mad."

                              "I may be mad."

"You look so, sitting out here in the rain
Studying genealogy with me
You never saw before. What will we come to
With all this pride of ancestry, we Yankees?
I think we're all mad. Tell me why we're here
Drawn into town about this cellar hole
Like wild geese on a lake before a storm?
What do we see in such a hole, I wonder."

"The Indians had a myth of Chicamoztoc,
Which means The Seven Caves that We Came out of.
This is the pit from which we Starks were digged."

"You must be learned. That's what you see in it?"

"And what do you see?"

                              "Yes, what *do* I see?
First let me look. I see raspberry vines——"

"Oh, if you're going to use your eyes, just hear
What *I* see. It's a little, little boy,
As pale and dim as a match flame in the sun;
He's groping in the cellar after jam,
He thinks it's dark and it's flooded with day-light."

"He's nothing. Listen. When I lean like this
I can make out old Grandsir Stark distinctly,—
With his pipe in his mouth and his brown jug—
Bless you, it isn't Grandsir Stark, it's Granny,
But the pipe's there and smoking and the jug.
She's after cider, the old girl, she's thirsty;
Here's hoping she gets her drink and gets out safely."

"Tell me about her. Does she look like me?"

"She should, shouldn't she, you're so many times
Over descended from her. I believe
She does look like you. Stay the way you are.
The nose is just the same, and so's the chin—
Making allowance, making due allowance."

"You poor, dear, great, great, great, great Granny!"

"See that you get her greatness right. Don't stint her."

"Yes, it's important, though you think it isn't.
I won't be teased. But see how wet I am."

"Yes, you must go; we can't stay here for ever.
But wait until I give you a hand up.
A bead of silver water more or less
Strung on your hair won't hurt your summer looks.
I wanted to try something with the noise
That the brook raises in the empty valley.
We have seen visions—now consult the voices.
Something I must have learned riding in trains
When I was young. I used the roar
To set the voices speaking out of it,
Speaking or singing, and the band-music playing.
Perhaps you have the art of what I mean.
I've never listened in among the sounds
That a brook makes in such a wild descent.
It ought to give a purer oracle."

"It's as you throw a picture on a screen:
The meaning of it all is out of you;
The voices give you what you wish to hear."

"Strangely, it's anything they wish to give."

"Then I don't know. It must be strange enough.
I wonder if it's not your make-believe.
What do you think you're like to hear to-day?"

"From the sense of our having been together—
But why take time for what I'm like to hear?
I'll tell you what the voices really say.
You will do very well right where you are
A little longer. I mustn't feel too hurried,
Or I can't give myself to hear the voices."

"Is this some trance you are withdrawing into?"

"You must be very still; you mustn't talk."

"I'll hardly breathe."

                    "The voices seem to say——"

"I'm waiting."

                    "Don't! The voices seem to say:
Call her Nausicaa, the unafraid
Of an acquaintance made adventurously."

"I let you say that—on consideration."

"I don't see very well how you can help it.
You want the truth. I speak but by the voices.
You see they know I haven't had your name,
Though what a name should matter between us——"

"I shall suspect——"

                    "Be good. The voices say:
Call her Nausicaa, and take a timber
That you shall find lies in the cellar charred
Among the raspberries, and hew and shape it

For a door-sill or other corner piece
In a new cottage on the ancient spot.
The life is not yet all gone out of it.
And come and make your summer dwelling here,
And perhaps she will come, still unafraid,
And sit before you in the open door
With flowers in her lap until they fade,
But not come in across the sacred sill———"

"I wonder where your oracle is tending.
You can see that there's something wrong with it,
Or it would speak in dialect. Whose voice
Does it purport to speak in? Not old Grandsir's
Nor Granny's, surely. Call up one of them.
They have best right to be heard in this place."
"You seem so partial to our great-grandmother
(Nine times removed. Correct me if I err.)
You will be likely to regard as sacred
Anything she may say. But let me warn you,
Folks in her day were given to plain speaking.
You think you'd best tempt her at such a time?"

"It rests with us always to cut her off."

"Well then, it's Granny speaking: 'I dunnow!
Mebbe I'm wrong to take it as I do.
There ain't no names quite like the old ones though,
Nor never will be to my way of thinking.
One mustn't bear too hard on the new comers,
But there's a dite too many of them for comfort.
I should feel easier if I could see
Most of the salt wherewith they're to be salted.
Son, you do as you're told! You take the timber—
It's as sound as the day when it was cut—
And begin over———' There, she'd better stop.
You can see what was troubling Granny, though.
But don't you think we sometimes make too much

Of the old stock? What counts is the ideals,
And those will bear some keeping still about."

"I can see we are going to be good friends."

"I like your 'going to be.' You said just now
It's going to rain."

                "I know, and it was raining.
I let you say all that. But I must go now."

"You let me say it? on consideration?
How shall we say good-bye in such a case?"

"How shall we?"

                "Will you leave the way to me?"

"No, I don't trust your eyes. You've said enough.
Now give me your hand up.—Pick me that flower."

"Where shall we meet again?"

                "Nowhere but here
Once more before we meet elsewhere."

                "In rain?"

"It ought to be in rain. Sometime in rain.
In rain to-morrow, shall we, if it rains?
But if we must, in sunshine." So she went.

THE HOUSEKEEPER

I let myself in at the kitchen door.

"It's you," *she said.* "I can't get up. Forgive me
Not answering your knock. I can no more
Let people in than I can keep them out.
I'm getting too old for my size, I tell them.
My fingers are about all I've the use of
So's to take any comfort. I can sew:
I help out with this beadwork what I can."

"That's a smart pair of pumps you're beading there.
Who are they for?"

                    "You mean?—-oh, for some miss.
I can't keep track of other people's daughters.
Lord, if I were to dream of everyone
Whose shoes I primped to dance in!"

                                        "And where's John?"

"Haven't you seen him? Strange what set you off
To come to his house when he's gone to yours.
You can't have passed each other. I know what:
He must have changed his mind and gone to Garlands.
He won't be long in that case. You can wait.
Though what good you can be, or anyone—
It's gone so far. You've heard? Estelle's run off."

"Yes, what's it all about? When did she go?"

"Two weeks since."

                              "She's in earnest, it appears."

"I'm sure she won't come back. She hiding somewhere.
I don't know where myself. John thinks I do.
He thinks I only have to say the word,
And she'll come back. But, bless you, I'm her mother—
I can't talk to her, and, Lord, if I could!"

"It will go hard with John. What will he do?
He can't find anyone to take her place."

"Oh, if you ask me that, what *will* he do?
He gets some sort of bakeshop meals together,
With me to sit and tell him everything,
What's wanted and how much and where it is.
But when I'm gone—of course I can't stay here:
Estelle's to take me when she's settled down.
He and I only hinder one another.
I tell them they can't get me through the door, though:
I've been built in here like a big church organ.
We've been here fifteen years."

                              "That's a long time
To live together and then pull apart.
How do you see him living when you're gone?
Two of you out will leave an empty house."

"I don't just see him living many years,
Left here with nothing but the furniture.
I hate to think of the old place when we're gone,
With the brook going by below the yard,
And no one here but hens blowing about.
If he could sell the place, but then, he can't:
No one will ever live on it again.
It's too run down. This is the last of it.
What I think he will do, is let things smash.
He'll sort of swear the time away. He's awful!

I never saw a man let family troubles
Make so much difference in his man's affairs.
He's just dropped everything. He's like a child.
I blame his being brought up by his mother.
He's got hay down that's been rained on three times.
He hoed a little yesterday for me:
I thought the growing things would do him good.
Something went wrong. I saw him throw the hoe
Sky-high with both hands. I can see it now—
Come here—I'll show you—in that apple tree.
That's no way for a man to do at his age:
He's fifty-five, you know, if he's a day."

"Aren't you afraid of him? What's that gun for?"

"Oh, that's been there for hawks since chicken-time.
John Hall touch me! Not if he knows his friends.
I'll say that for him, John's no threatener
Like some men folk. No one's afraid of him;
All is, he's made up his mind not to stand
What he has got to stand."

                                        "Where is Estelle?
Couldn't one talk to her? What does she say?
You say you don't know where she is."

                                        "Nor want to!
She thinks if it was bad to live with him,
It must be right to leave him."

                                        "Which is wrong!"

"Yes, but he should have married her."

                                        "I know."

"The strain's been too much for her all these years:
I can't explain it any other way.

It's different with a man, at least with John:
He knows he's kinder than the run of men.
Better than married ought to be as good
As married—that's what he has always said.
I know the way he's felt—but all the same!"

"I wonder why he doesn't marry her
And end it."

           "Too late now: she wouldn't have him.
He's given her time to think of something else.
That's his mistake. The dear knows my interest
Has been to keep the thing from breaking up.
This is a good home: I don't ask for better.
But when I've said, 'Why shouldn't they be married?'
He'd say, 'Why should they?' no more words than
    that."

"And after all why should they? John's been fair
I take it. What was his was always hers.
There was no quarrel about property."

"Reason enough, there was no property.
A friend or two as good as own the farm,
Such as it is. It isn't worth the mortgage."

"I mean Estelle has always held the purse."

"The rights of that are harder to get at.
I guess Estelle and I have filled the purse.
'Twas we let him have money, not he us.
John's a bad farmer. I'm not blaming him.
Take it year in, year out, he doesn't make much.
We came here for a home for me, you know,
Estelle to do the housework for the board
Of both of us. But look how it turns out:
She seems to have the housework, and besides

Half of the outdoor work, though as for that,
He'd say she does it more because she likes it.
You see our pretty things are all outdoors.
Our hens and cows and pigs are always better
Than folks like us have any business with.
Farmers around twice as well off as we
Haven't as good. They don't go with the farm.
One thing you can't help liking about John,
He's fond of nice things—too fond, some would say.
But Estelle don't complain: she's like him there.
She wants our hens to be the best there are.
You never saw this room before a show,
Full of lank, shivery, half-drowned birds
In separate coops, having their plumage done.
The smell of wet feathers in the heat!
You spoke of John's not being safe to stay with.
You don't know what a gentle lot we are:
We wouldn't hurt a hen! You ought to see us
Moving a flock of hens from place to place,
We're not allowed to take them upside down,
All we can hold together by the legs.
Two at a time's the rule, one on each arm,
No matter how far and how many times
We have to go."

                    "You mean that's John's idea."

"And we live up to it; or I don't know
What childishness he wouldn't give way to.
He manages to keep the upper hand
On his own farm. He's boss. But as to hens:
We fence our flowers in and the hens range.
Nothing's too good for them. We say it pays.
John likes to tell the offers he has had,
Twenty for this cock, twenty-five for that.
He never takes the money. If they're worth
That much to sell, they're worth as much to keep.

Bless you, it's all expense, though. Reach me down
The little tin box on the cupboard shelf,
The upper shelf, the tin box. That's the one.
I'll show you. Here you are."

                    "What's this?"

                              "A bill—
For fifty dollars for one Langshang cock—
Receipted. And the cock is in the yard."

"Not in a glass case, then?"

                    "He'd need a tall one:
He can eat off a barrel from the ground.
He's been in a glass case, as you may say,
The Crystal Palace, London. He's imported.
John bought him, and we paid the bill with beads—
Wampum, I call it. Mind, we don't complain.
But you see, don't you, we take care of him."

"And like it, too. It makes it all the worse."

"It seems as if. And that's not all: he's helpless
In ways that I can hardly tell you of.
Sometimes he gets possessed to keep accounts
To see where all the money goes so fast.
You know how men will be ridiculous.
But it's just fun the way he gets bedeviled—
If he's untidy now, what will he be——?"

"It makes it all the worse. You must be blind."

"Estelle's the one. You needn't talk to me."

"Can't you and I get to the root of it?

What's the real trouble? What will satisfy her?"

"It's as I say: she's turned from him, that's all."

"But why, when she's well off? Is it the neighbours,
Being cut off from friends?"

                        "We have our friends.
That isn't it. Folks aren't afraid of us."

"She's let it worry her. You stood the strain,
And you're her mother."

                        "But I didn't always.
I didn't relish it along at first.
But I got wonted to it. And besides—
John said I was too old to have grandchildren.
But what's the use of talking when it's done?
She won't come back—it's worse than that—she can't."

"Why do you speak like that? What do you know?
What do you mean?—she's done harm to herself?"

"I mean she's married—married someone else."

"Oho, oho!"

                    "You don't believe me."

                          "Yes, I do,
Only too well. I knew there must be something!
So that was all back. She's bad, that's all!"

"Bad to get married when she had the chance?"

"Nonsense! See what she's done! But who, who——"

"Who'd marry her straight out of such a mess?
Say it right out—no matter for her mother.
The man was found. I'd better name no names.
John himself won't imagine who he is."

"Then it's all up. I think I'll get away.
You'll be expecting John. I pity Estelle;
I suppose she deserves some pity, too.
You ought to have the kitchen to yourself
To break it to him. You may have the job."

"You needn't think you're going to get away.
John's almost here. I've had my eye on someone
Coming down Ryan's Hill. I thought 'twas him.
Here he is now. This box! Put it away.
And this bill."

                    "What's the hurry? He'll unhitch."

"No, he won't, either. He'll just drop the reins.
And turn Doll out to pasture, rig and all.
She won't get far before the wheels hang up
On something—there's no harm. See, there he is!
My, but he looks as if he must have heard!"

John threw the door wide but he didn't enter.
"How are you, neighbour? Just the man I'm after.
Isn't it Hell?" *he said.* "I want to know.
Come out here if you want to hear me talk.
I'll talk to you, old woman, afterward.
I've got some news that maybe isn't news.
What are they trying to do to me, these two?"

"Do go along with him and stop his shouting."
She raised her voice against the closing door:
"Who wants to hear your news, you—dreadful fool?"

THE FEAR

A lantern light from deeper in the barn
Shone on a man and woman in the door
And threw their lurching shadows on a house
Near by, all dark in every glossy window.
A horse's hoof pawed once the hollow floor,
And the back of the gig they stood beside
Moved in a little. The man grasped a wheel,
The woman spoke out sharply, "Whoa; stand still!"
"I saw it just as plain as a white plate,"
She said, "as the light on the dashboard ran
Along the bushes at the roadside—a man's face.
You *must* have seen it too."

                                        "I didn't see it.
Are you sure——"

                        "Yes, I'm sure!"

                                  "—it was a face?"

"Joel, I'll have to look. I can't go in,
I can't, and leave a thing like that unsettled.
Doors locked and curtains drawn will make no difference.
I always have felt strange when we come home
To the dark house after so long an absence,
And the key rattled loudly into place
Seemed to warn someone to be getting out
At one door as we entered at another.
What if I'm right, and someone all the time—
Don't hold my arm!"

                          "I say it's someone passing."

"You speak as if this were a travelled road.
You forget where we are. What is beyond
That he'd be going to or coming from
At such an hour of night, and on foot too.
What was he standing still for in the bushes?"

"It's not so very late—it's only dark.
There's more in it than you're inclined to say.
Did he look like——?"

　　　　　　　　　　　"He looked like anyone.
I'll never rest to-night unless I know.
Give me the lantern."

　　　　　　　　　　　"You don't want the lantern."

She pushed past him and got it for herself.

"You're not to come," she said. "This is my business.
If the time's come to face it, I'm the one
To put it the right way. He'd never dare—
Listen! He kicked a stone. Hear that, hear that!
He's coming toward us. Joel, *go* in—please.
Hark!—I don't hear him now. But please go in."

"In the first place you can't make me believe it's——"

"It is—or someone else he's sent to watch.
And now's the time to have it out with him
While we know definitely where he is.
Let him get off and he'll be everywhere
Around us, looking out of trees and bushes
Till I sha'n't dare to set a foot outdoors.
And I can't stand it. Joel, let me go!"

"But it's nonsense to think he'd care enough."

"You mean you couldn't understand his caring.
Oh, but you see he hadn't had enough—
Joel, I won't—I won't—I promise you.
We mustn't say hard things. You mustn't either."

"I'll be the one, if anybody goes!
But you give him the advantage with this light.
What couldn't he do to us standing here!
And if to see was what he wanted, why
He has seen all there was to see and gone."

He appeared to forget to keep his hold,
But advanced with her as she crossed the grass.

"What do you want?" she cried out to all the dark.
She stretched up tall to overlook the light
That hung in both hands hot against her skirt.

"There's no one; so you're wrong," he said.

                                    "There is.—
What do you want?" she cried, and then herself
Was startled when an answer really came.

"Nothing." It came from well along the road.

She reached a hand to Joel for support:
The smell of scorching woollen made her faint.

"What are you doing round this house at night?"

"Nothing." A pause: there seemed no more to say.

And then the voice again: "You seem afraid.
I saw by the way you whipped up the horse.
I'll just come forward in the lantern light
And let you see."

                "Yes, do.—Joel, go back!"

She stood her ground against the noisy steps
That came on, but her body rocked a little.

"You see," the voice said.

                      "Oh." She looked and looked.

"You don't see—I've a child here by the hand."

"What's a child doing at this time of night——?"

"Out walking. Every child should have the memory
Of at least one long-after-bedtime walk.
What, son?"

               "Then I should think you'd try to find
Somewhere to walk——"

               "The highway as it happens—
We're stopping for the fortnight down at Dean's."

"But if that's all—Joel—you realize—
You won't think anything. You understand?
You understand that we have to be careful.
This is a very, very lonely place.
Joel!" She spoke as if she couldn't turn.
The swinging lantern lengthened to the ground,
It touched, it struck it, clattered and went out.

THE SELF-SEEKER

"Willis, I don't want you here to-day:
The lawyer's coming for the company.
I'm going to sell my soul, or, rather, feet.
Five hundred dollars for the pair, you know."

"With you the feet have nearly been the soul;
And if you're going to sell them to the devil,
I want to see you do it. When's he coming?"

"I half suspect you knew, and came on purpose
To try to help me drive a better bargain."

"Well, if it's true! Yours are no common feet.
The lawyer don't know what it is he's buying:
So many miles you might have walked you won't walk.
You haven't run your forty orchids down.
What does he think?—How *are* the blessed feet?
The doctor's sure you're going to walk again?"

"He thinks I'll hobble. It's both legs and feet."

"They must be terrible—I mean to look at."

"I haven't dared to look at them uncovered.
Through the bed blankets I remind myself
Of a starfish laid out with rigid points."

"The wonder is it hadn't been your head."

"It's hard to tell you how I managed it.
When I saw the shaft had me by the coat,
I didn't try too long to pull away,
Or fumble for my knife to cut away,
I just embraced the shaft and rode it out—

Till Weiss shut off the water in the wheel-pit.
That's how I think I didn't lose my head.
But my legs got their knocks against the ceiling."

"Awful. Why didn't they throw off the belt
Instead of going clear down in the wheel-pit?"

"They say some time was wasted on the belt—
Old streak of leather—doesn't love me much
Because I make him spit fire at my knuckles,
The way Ben Franklin used to make the kite-string.
That must be it. Some days he won't stay on.
That day a woman couldn't coax him off.
He's on his rounds now with his tail in his mouth
Snatched right and left across the silver pulleys.
Everything goes the same without me there.
You can hear the small buzz saws whine, the big saw
Caterwaul to the hills around the village
As they both bite the wood. It's all our music.
One ought as a good villager to like it.
No doubt it has a sort of prosperous sound,
And it's our life."

                    "Yes, when it's not our death."

"You make that sound as if it wasn't so
With everything. What we live by we die by.
I wonder where my lawyer is. His train's in.
I want this over with; I'm hot and tired."

"You're getting ready to do something foolish."

"Watch for him, will you, Will? You let him in.
I'd rather Mrs. Corbin didn't know;
I've boarded here so long, she thinks she owns me.
You're bad enough to manage without her."

"And I'm going to be worse instead of better.
You've got to tell me how far this is gone:
Have you agreed to any price?"

                                  "Five hundred.
Five hundred—five—five! One, two, three, four, five.
You needn't look at me."

                               "I don't believe you."

"I told you, Willis, when you first came in.
Don't you be hard on me. I have to take
What I can get. You see they have the feet,
Which gives them the advantage in the trade.
I can't get back the feet in any case."

"But your flowers, man, you're selling out your
    flowers."

"Yes, that's one way to put it—all the flowers
Of every kind everywhere in this region
For the next forty summers—call it forty.
But I'm not selling those, I'm giving them,
They never earned me so much as one cent:
Money can't pay me for the loss of them.
No, the five hundred was the sum they named
To pay the doctor's bill and tide me over.
It's that or fight, and I don't want to fight—
I just want to get settled in my life,
Such as it's going to be, and know the worst,
Or best—it may not be so bad. The firm
Promise me all the shooks I want to nail."

"But what about your flora of the valley?"

"You have me there. But that—you didn't think
That was worth money to me? Still I own
It goes against me not to finish it
For the friends it might bring me. By the way,

I had a letter from Burroughs—did I tell you?—
About my *Cyprepedium reginæ;*
He says it's not reported so far north.
There! there's the bell. He's rung. But you go down
And bring him up, and don't let Mrs. Corbin.—
Oh, well, we'll soon be through with it. I'm tired."

Willis brought up besides the Boston lawyer
A little barefoot girl who in the noise
Of heavy footsteps in the old frame house,
And baritone importance of the lawyer,
Stood for a while unnoticed with her hands
Shyly behind her.

                           "Well, and how is Mister—"

The lawyer was already in his satchel
As if for papers that might bear the name
He hadn't at command. "You must excuse me,
I dropped in at the mill and was detained."

"Looking round, I suppose," said Willis.

                                                   "Yes,
Well, yes."

                   "Hear anything that might prove useful?"

The Broken One saw Anne, "Why, here is Anne.
What do you want, dear? Come, stand by the bed;
Tell me what is it?" Anne just wagged her dress
With both hands held behind her. "Guess," she said.

"Oh, guess which hand? My, my! Once on a time
I know a lovely way to tell for certain
By looking in the ears. But I forget it.
Er, let me see. I think I'll take the right.
That's sure to be right even if it's wrong.

Come, hold it out. Don't change.—A Ram's Horn
    orchid!
A Ram's Horn! What would I have got, I wonder,
If I had chosen left. Hold out the left.
Another Ram's Horn! Where did you find those,
Under what beech tree, on what woodchuck's knoll?"

Anne looked at the large lawyer at her side,
And thought she wouldn't venture on so much.

"Were there no others?"

                                "There were four or five.
I knew you wouldn't let me pick them all."

"I wouldn't—so I wouldn't. You're the girl!
You see Anne has her lesson learned by heart."

"I wanted there should be some there next year."

"Of course you did. You left the rest for seed,
And for the backwoods woodchuck. You're the girl!
A Ram's Horn orchid seedpod for a woodchuck
Sounds something like. Better than farmer's beans
To a discriminating appetite,
Though the Ram's Horn is seldom to be had
In bushel lots—doesn't come on the market.
But, Anne, I'm troubled; have you told me all?
You're hiding something. That's as bad as lying.
You ask this lawyer man. And it's not safe
With a lawyer at hand to find you out.
Nothing is hidden from some people, Anne.
You don't tell me that where you found a Ram's Horn
You didn't find a Yellow Lady's Slipper.
What did I tell you? What? I'd blush, I would.
Don't you defend yourself. If it was there,
Where is it now, the Yellow Lady's Slipper?"

"Well, wait—it's common—it's too *common*."

                                        "Common?
The Purple Lady's Slipper's commoner."

"I didn't bring a Purple Lady's Slipper
To *You*—to you I mean—they're both too common."

The lawyer gave a laugh among his papers
As if with some idea that she had scored.

"I've broken Anne of gathering bouquets.
It's not fair to the child. It can't be helped though:
Pressed into service means pressed out of shape.
Somehow I'll make it right with her—she'll see.
She's going to do my scouting in the field,
Over stone walls and all along a wood
And by a river bank for water flowers,
The floating Heart, with small leaf like a heart,
And at the *sinus* under water a fist
Of little fingers all kept down but one,
And that thrust up to blossom in the sun
As if to say, 'You! You're the Heart's desire.'
Anne has a way with flowers to take the place
Of that she's lost: she goes down on one knee
And lifts their faces by the chin to hers
And says their names, and leaves them where
     they are."

The lawyer wore a watch the case of which
Was cunningly devised to make a noise
Like a small pistol when he snapped it shut
At such a time as this. He snapped it now.

"Well, Anne, go, dearie. Our affair will wait.
The lawyer man is thinking of his train.
He wants to give me lots and lots of money
Before he goes, because I hurt myself,
And it may take him I don't know how long.

But put our flowers in water first. Will, help her:
The pitcher's too full for her. There's no cup?
Just hook them on the inside of the pitcher.
Now run.—Get out your documents! You see
I have to keep on the good side of Anne.
I'm a great boy to think of number one.
And you can't blame me in the place I'm in.
Who will take care of my necessities
Unless I do?"

                            "A pretty interlude,"
The lawyer said. "I'm sorry, but my train—
Luckily terms are all agreed upon.
You only have to sign your name. Right—there."

"You, Will, stop making faces. Come round here
Where you can't make them. What is it you want?
I'll put you out with Anne. Be good or go."

"You don't mean you will sign that thing unread?"

"Make yourself useful then, and read it for me.
Isn't it something I have seen before?"

"You'll find it is. Let your friend look at it."

"Yes, but all that takes time, and I'm as much
In haste to get it over with as you.
But read it, read it. That's right, draw the curtain:
Half the time I don't know what's troubling me.—
What do you say, Will? Don't you be a fool,
You! crumpling folkses legal documents.
Out with it if you've any real objection."

"Five hundred dollars!"

                          "What would you think right?"

"A thousand wouldn't be a cent too much;
You know it, Mr. Lawyer. The sin is

Accepting anything before he knows
Whether he's ever going to walk again.
It smells to me like a dishonest trick."

"I think—I think—from what I heard to-day—
And saw myself—he would be ill-advised——"

"What did you hear, for instance?" Willis said.

"Now the place where the accident occurred—"

The Broken One was twisted in his bed.
"This is between you two apparently.
Where I come in is what I want to know.
You stand up to it like a pair of cocks.
Go outdoors if you want to fight. Spare me.
When you come back, I'll have the papers signed.
Will pencil do? Then, please, your fountain pen.
One of you hold my head up from the pillow."

Willis flung off the bed. "I wash my hands—
I'm no match—no, and don't pretend to be——"

The lawyer gravely capped his fountain pen.
"You're doing the wise thing: you won't regret it.
We're very sorry for you."

                                   Willis sneered:
"Who's *we?*—some stockholders in Boston?
I'll go outdoors, by gad, and won't come back."

"Willis, bring Anne back with you when you come.
Yes. Thanks for caring. Don't mind Will: he's savage.
He thinks you ought to pay me for my flowers.
You don't know what I mean about the flowers.
Don't stop to try to now. You'll miss your train.
Good-bye." He flung his arms around his face.

THE WOOD-PILE

Out walking in the frozen swamp one grey day
I paused and said, "I will turn back from here.
No, I will go on farther—and we shall see."
The hard snow held me, save where now and then
One foot went down. The view was all in lines
Straight up and down of tall slim trees
Too much alike to mark or name a place by
So as to say for certain I was here
Or somewhere else: I was just far from home.
A small bird flew before me. He was careful
To put a tree between us when he lighted,
And say no word to tell me who he was
Who was so foolish as to think what *he* thought.
He thought that I was after him for a feather—
The white one in his tail; like one who takes
Everything said as personal to himself.
One flight out sideways would have undeceived him.
And then there was a pile of wood for which
I forgot him and let his little fear
Carry him off the way I might have gone,
Without so much as wishing him good-night.
He went behind it to make his last stand.
It was a cord of maple, cut and split
And piled—and measured, four by four by eight.
And not another like it could I see.
No runner tracks in this year's snow looped near it.
And it was older sure than this year's cutting,
Or even last year's or the year's before.
The wood was grey and the bark warping off it
And the pile somewhat sunken. Clematis
Had wound strings round and round it like a bundle.
What held it though on one side was a tree

Still growing, and on one a stake and prop,
These latter about to fall. I thought that only
Someone who lived in turning to fresh tasks
Could so forget his handiwork on which
He spent himself, the labour of his axe,
And leave it there far from a useful fireplace
To warm the frozen swamp as best it could
With the slow smokeless burning of decay.

GOOD HOURS

I had for my winter evening walk—
No one at all with whom to talk,
But I had the cottages in a row
Up to their shining eyes in snow.

And I thought I had the folk within:
I had the sound of a violin;
I had a glimpse through curtain laces
Of youthful forms and youthful faces.

I had such company outward bound.
I went till there were no cottages found.
I turned and repented, but coming back
I saw no window but that was black.

Over the snow my creaking feet
Disturbed the slumbering village street
Like profanation, by your leave,
At ten o'clock of a winter eve.

AFTERWORD

Farness and Depth

In his very long life, Robert Frost saw huge changes
overtake poetry in English. Young Robert Frost had
just entered Dartmouth College in 1892, when Alfred,
Lord Tennyson died; his own death in 1963, at eighty-
eight, preceded that of Sylvia Plath (his grandchil-
dren's contemporary) by only two weeks. The poems
in this book, published when Frost was turning forty,
brought to its destiny a revolution in poetry in whose
inventive vanguard Frost soon found himself, along
with Ezra Pound, T. S. Eliot, Wallace Stevens, William
Carlos Williams, and the rest. American speech would
henceforward bring new intonations to the long-estab-
lished vocal traditions of European poetry. Whitman,
who had so brashly incited the American eagle to soar,
and Emily Dickinson, who had peered into the intima-
cies of the American soul, opened doors for our po-
etry in the late nineteenth century that, in the early
years of the twentieth century, were threatening to
close again. Now in 1914, Frost, by virtue of his first
two books, especially *North of Boston*, had just let our
poetry run free in the common language while re-
taining the ancient prosodical magic of English verse
as part of his poetic carriage.

"The fact is the sweetest dream that labor knows"—
that prophetic line from "Mowing"—is one of the
most mysterious and most poignant lines in all poetry.
It was the signal to himself that Frost had found re-

sources in the facts of American life and in the sweetness of American language that would enlarge and deepen the poetry written in America thereafter, and therefore eventually deepen Americans' understanding of themselves. Although Frost had already begun to make his name by the time he returned from old England to New England in February 1915, by the time he got home he already had a considerable part of a third book written, including two poems called "Birches" and "The Road Not Taken." These two unforgettable poems, along with another called "The Sound of Trees," were published in *The Atlantic Monthly* in August 1915, along with a powerful appreciation of Frost's poetry by the English critic and editor Edward Garnett, the same foresighted evaluator who had encouraged the early creativity of Joseph Conrad and D. H. Lawrence, and whose wife, Constance, had translated Tolstoy and Dostoevsky into English. Garnett knew a classic writer when he read one. *Mountain Interval*, published promptly in America in 1916, would enlarge on the lyricism of *A Boy's Will*. It comprised not only poems like "Birches" and "The Road Not Taken," but "The Oven Bird," "An Old Man's Winter Night," and the horrifying "Out, Out—". *Mountain Interval* also contained some of Frost's most poignant upland poems, such as "Snow" and "The Hill Wife"—poems that deal plainly with the oddities and remoteness of country people.

Frost is one of the great poets of loneliness, especially the loneliness of women. In his first three volumes, he cast back in memory to the late years of the nineteenth century, years when New England's country primacy had been drained away by our westward migration to more fertile soils. Frost had stayed east with his family on a farm in Derry, New Hampshire, and had discovered, by the ways of talking that his New

Hampshire neighbors used, something of what had been left behind in loneliness when America moved toward its manifest destiny across the Great Plains. Unfortunately, *Mountain Interval* did not meet with the acclaim that had welcomed *North of Boston*. Having exhausted his savings and his nerve, Frost was constrained to go back to his pre-England ways of supporting his family, a combination of teaching at Amherst College and a little farming in summers at Franconia, New Hampshire.

Now that he had settled back in his native land with the confidence of a man who had finally learned how to write the poems he was born to, Frost would also find the confidence to declare himself outright in a variety of wisdom poems, reflections on the human situation, rather different from anything in his first two books. To my mind, these poems, many of them sonnets, amount to his most profound achievement. In them he seized upon strict form in order to make his point. In addition to those poems in *Mountain Interval*—and poems like "Design" (1923), which he later claimed he began in 1912, and "To Earthward" (1923) or "Not Far Out Nor In Deep," which first saw print in 1934, "Provide, Provide," of the same year, and "The Gift Outright" and "The Most of It" (1942), or "The Draft Horse," which, whenever it was begun (perhaps 1920), he did not publish until 1962, and two of his most profound longer poems, "West-Running Brook" (1928) and "Directive" (1946)—Frost's most startlingly challenging wisdom poems took their shape from the middle age of his poetic life, his fortieth to his seventieth year. They were published in the books that he released between 1923 and 1942, four of which won Pulitzer Prizes. In these years set out to explore the possibilities of strict English verse forms: how the discipline of rhythmic speech could help fathom the mystery of life on the planet. Though he had unleashed back-country

American speech into *blank* verse, he could never join Walt Whitman and Carl Sandburg or William Carlos Williams in the sweeping or intimate gestures of *free* verse. He preferred (as did Eliot and Wallace Stevens) to release the particular flavor of his speech only within the frame of predetermined form. He once told me that there was only one poem in his entire published work that fell into the free verse category. He claimed, in a letter to *The Amherst Student*, to drive a certain strength and stability from reliance on form: "Anyone who has achieved the least form to be sure of it, is lost to the larger excruciations. I think it must stroke faith the right way."

Yet his faith was not facile or hollow. As he wrote in "The Oven Bird,"

> The bird would cease and be as other birds
> But that he knows in singing not to sing.
> The question that he frames in all but words
> Is what to make of a diminished thing.

Or of being left behind? Or of the importance of hate in the world?

> Some say the world will end in fire,
> Some say in ice.
> From what I've tasted of desire
> I hold with those who favor fire.
> But if it had to perish twice
> I think I know enough of hate
> To say that for destruction ice
> Is also great
> And would suffice.
>
> —"Fire and Ice," 1920

Beyond his formal intentions, however, two very special qualities enriched his work from beginning to end.

One was his understanding and affection for the ways
in which women expressed themselves, as in a hundred
examples from "A Servant to Servants" and "The
Death of the Hired Man" to "The Subverted Flower"
and "The Silken Tent." The second was his willingness
to accept fate and chance as part of the great adventure
of human life, a willingness that Lionel Trilling in a
notorious tribute called "terrifying." Randall Jarrell,
who shared Trilling's view but stated it more elo-
quently, has written better than any other poet about
the inner quality of Frost's poetry, but critics have writ-
ten very well too, notably Elizabeth Shepley Sergeant
(1960), Reuben Brower (1963), Richard Poirier (1977),
and William H. Pritchard (1984), whose introduction to
this volume anyone can learn much from. If, however,
I were to pick one single piece of extended writing
about Frost to clarify the balance between his mysteri-
ous personality and his poetic achievement, it would be
"Toward the 'Knowable' Frost," the last chapter of a
book titled *Robert Frost Himself* (1986) by his last edi-
tor, Stanley Burnshaw.

I knew Frost in person pretty well, well enough so
that it has taken me forty years to get over it. He was
the most interesting man I have ever encountered: a
sublime, witty, and resourceful talker who talked to
tease out the world's secrets without a compulsion to
explain them—as in Keats's famous plea for negative
capability. Randall Jarrell, writing soon after Frost's
death, characterized the unmistakable sound of Frost's
voice, whether you encountered it in life, in re-
cordings, or on the page, where he made it live on
after his death:

> In the end he talked as naturally as he breathed:
> for as long as you got to listen you were sharing
> Frost's life. What came to you in that deep
> grainy voice—a voice that made other voices

sound thin or abstract—was half a natural
physiological process and half a work of art: it
was as if Frost dreamed aloud and the dream
were a poem. Was what he said right or wrong?
It seemed irrelevant. In the same way, whether
Frost himself was good or bad seemed irrele-
vant—he was there and you accepted him.

After Frost died and the posthumous biographies
started coming out, those who had not known him fell
into a wrangle: whether Frost in life was a "good
man" or a "real monster." Such a debate belongs
more to the annals of celebrity than to those of po-
etry, because Frost had become a celebrity during
his lifetime; but those who want to understand Frost
the Man now have only the biographies—nearly all of
them unsatisfactory—to inform them. The early ones,
those published during his lifetime, had showed them-
selves perhaps too eager to hero-worship the man
whose voice they had heard and succumbed to. The
definitive biography, the indignant three-volume work
written over a period of years by Lawrance Thompson
(with the posthumous assistance of Roy Winnick Jr.),
shows what a terrible mistake Frost had made in
choosing his own biographer and then living on for
many years. Thompson, through overexposure and ac-
cident, came to loathe Frost and turn his three-volume
biography into a three-volume act of revenge, sup-
ported by decades of obsessive note-taking. Unfortu-
nately, the huge array of useful fact in Thompson's
work has overweighed its knotted mass of grievance
and continues to keep a heavy finger on the scales.
Thompson seemed unable to forgive Frost for having
been one who, in his personal life, was among the
unluckiest of poets, if in his public life one of the most
successful. Frost during his lifetime lost two children
to death in early childhood, another to insanity, an-

other to death after childbirth, and still another (after the death of Frost's wife, Elinor) to suicide. Like any sensitive man who suffers, Frost sometimes blamed himself for his misfortune; but Thompson took Frost too seriously in this self-laceration and set himself up as the poet's judge rather than as his explainer. Frost's human reputation will probably never recover.

For me, however, the most satisfying and most imaginative of all the biographical books about Frost is also the most modest: John Evangelist Walsh's partial biography titled *Into My Own: The English Years of Robert Frost* (1988). This was written by a man who, having not known Frost, had no interest in loving or hating the man, but only in discovering how the great poems had been written. Walsh was able better than anyone else, by listening truly to the poems themselves and by conducting original biographical research, to recreate the ways, times, and places in which Robert Frost found himself during the years in which *A Boy's Will* and *North of Boston* took shape.

Late in Frost's life, within the memory of people in middle age today, he became more and less than a famous poet: he became a sort of national totem. His humor had a great deal to do with it: like Mark Twain, Frost attracted a huge public by the charm and informality of his talk; and as with Mark Twain, a darkness lay beneath the humor. (Thus, the quip he voiced toward the end of his life: "Forgive, O Lord, my little jokes on Thee /And I'll forgive Thy great big one on me.") Frost attained a larger audience during his lifetime than any serious poet who had ever preceded him in America. After John F. Kennedy chose him to read a poem at his presidential inauguration in 1961, and after Frost, in the last year of his life, traveled to Russia and, speaking as a poet, confronted Nikita Khrushchev on the Black Sea Coast of Georgia, he came to be regarded as a sort of holy idiot, possibly senile. It was his own fault: in his later years some of his poetry was written—or at least performed on public platforms—with the clear intention of entertaining huge audiences. These poems, knowingly amusing at their best, sometimes a little cheaply, strike a posture of know-nothing smugness that seems less than worthy of their author. They put Frost in danger of outliving his own popularity.

After *Steeple Bush* (1947), the intelligentsia had begun to turn against him, and by the 1950s many of those associated with universities (like those who taught me at Harvard in the 1940s) had come to prefer the hieratic, ceremonious verse of T. S. Eliot. Frost didn't like that one bit. In 1934 he wrote to his daughter Lesley, "I confess I have several times forgotten my dignity in speaking in public of Eliot." I can recall his saying, perhaps twenty-five years later, "Eliot doesn't want people to understand him. I want people to understand me: I want 'em to understand me wrong."

He got his wish. For a considerable time Americans tended to regard Frost as the other bookend to match Norman Rockwell as a sly grandfatherly figure whose work could be counted on to convey the values of traditional American country life. But after Frost's death, and after all the silly furor about whether or not he was a monster abated, readers were ineluctably faced with the poetry itself. The seductive voice of the old man no longer distracted us. The poetry somehow will not go away, and keeps surprising us with its mysteries:

> For I have promises to keep,
> And miles to go before I sleep
> And miles to go before I sleep.

> Two roads diverged in a wood, but I
> I took the one less traveled by,
> And that has made all the difference.

Everyone thinks he or she knows what these *words*
mean—but it proves a good deal harder to understand,
or to puzzle out, just what it is the poems are getting
at. To this day, in classrooms and libraries, students
and teachers alike struggle with that sweetly puzzling
poetry: the enigmatic meaning concealed behind sim-
ple language, the paradoxical and surprising meaning
couched in traditional form. Poetry is unruly, unpre-
dictable: it does not operate in the same ways as prose.
As Frost himself famously wrote:

> The figure a poem makes. It begins in delight
> and ends in wisdom. The figure is the same as
> for love. No one can really hold that the ecstasy
> should be static and stand still in one place. It
> begins in delight, it inclines to the impulse, it
> assumes direction with the first line laid down,
> it runs a course of lucky events, and ends in a
> clarification of life—not necessarily a great clari-
> fication, such as sects and cults are founded on,
> but in a momentary stay against confusion. It
> has denouement.

The truths a Frost poem reveals are poetic truths,
not social slogans or ethical bromides. Readers of
Frost's poetry in the decades since his death have
gradually learned better to read and understand what
he left us. Poets as diverse as the Russian Joseph
Brodsky and the Caribbean Derek Walcott, critics as
diverse as our contemporaries Helen Vendler and
Greg Kuzma, have found Frost's poetry lighting up
our understanding in ways that were not originally
comprehended—or not at least by its readers. Their
author set them in motion and, departing, left it up to
them to keep kicking down the years. Their journey
is getting more interesting all the time. Frost hasn't
lost his ginger yet. His farness and his depth were

never better demonstrated than in a poem of 1936 called "Not Out Far Nor In Deep":

> The people along the sand
> All turn and look one way.
> They turn their back on the land.
> They look at the sea all day.
>
> As long as it tries to pass
> A ship keeps raising its hull.
> The wetter ground like glass
> Reflects a standing gull.
>
> The land may vary more;
> But wherever the truth may be—
> The water comes ashore,
> And the people look at the sea.
>
> They cannot look out far.
> They cannot look in deep.
> But when was that ever a bar
> To any watch they keep?

—Peter Davison

NOTE

The texts used here are the first English editions of *A Boy's Will* (1913) and *North of Boston* (1914). The first American editions are identical. In later editions and in *The Poetry of Robert Frost*, ed., E. C. Lathem (1969), the glosses to *A Boy's Will* and the tripartite division of the volume were removed, as were three poems, "Asking for Roses," "In Equal Sacrifice," and "Spoils of the Dead." "The Pasture" has been restored to Frost's original placement of it as an epigraph to *North of Boston*.

Bibliography of Critical Works

With reference to *A Boy's Will* and *North of Boston*, the following biographical and critical studies are of interest:

George Bagby. *Robert Frost and the Book of Nature* (Knoxville: University of Tennessee Press, 1993).

Joseph Brodsky, Seamus Heaney, and Derek Walcott. *Homage to Robert Frost* (New York: Farrar, Straus and Giroux, 1996).

Stanley Burnshaw. *Robert Frost Himself* (New York: G. Braziller, 1986).

Edwin H. Cady and Louis J. Budd, eds. *On Frost* (Durham: Duke University Press, 1991).

Robert Faggen. *Robert Frost and the Challenge of Darwinism* (Ann Arbor: University of Michigan Press, 1997).

Philip L. Gerber, ed. *Critical Essays on Robert Frost* (Boston: G. K. Hall, 1982).

Ed Ingebretsen. *Robert Frost's Star in a Stone-boat: A Grammar of Belief* (San Francisco: Catholic Scholars Press, 1994).

Randall Jarrell, ed. *No Other Book: Selected Essays* (New York: HarperCollins, 1999).

John Kemp. *Robert Frost and New England: The Poet as Regionalist* (Princeton: Princeton University Press, 1979).

Frank Lentricchia. *Modernist Quartet* (Cambridge: Cambridge University Press, 1994).

Jeffrey Meyers. *Robert Frost: A Biography* (Boston: Houghton Mifflin, 1996).

George Monteiro. *Robert Frost and the New England Renaissance* (Lexington: University Press of Kentucky, 1988).

Judith Oster. *Toward Robert Frost: The Reader and the Poet* (Athens: University of Georgia Press, 1991).

Jay Parini. *Robert Frost: A Life* (New York: Henry Holt, 1999).

Richard Poirier. *Robert Frost: The Work of Knowing* (Palo Alto: Stanford University Press, 1990).

William H. Pritchard. *Frost: A Literary Life Reconsidered*, 2d ed. (Amherst: University of Massachusetts Press, 1993).

Donald Sheehy. *Poems, Life, Legacy,* CD-ROM (New York: Henry Holt, 1997).

Lawrance Thompson, ed. *Selected Letters of Robert Frost* (Holt, Rinehart and Winston, 1964).

Lawrance Thompson and R. H. Winnick. *Robert Frost: A Biography*, one-volume ed. (New York: Holt, Rinehart and Winston, 1981).

Lionel Trilling. *The Moral Obligation to Be Intelligent: Selected Essays* (New York: Farrar, Straus, and Giroux, 2000).

John Evangelist Wash. *Into My Own: The English Years of Robert Frost 1912–1915* (New York: Grove Press, 1988).

America's Poetry from Signet Classics

SPOON RIVER ANTHOLOGY by Edgar Lee Masters
A notorious success when first published in 1915, Masters'
collection of free verse monologues is populated by 200
former inhabitants of an imagined Midwestern town,
speaking their epitaphs from beyond the grave. This is a
triumphant proclamation of the American Spirit, at once
moving, literate and down home.

THE WASTE LAND & Other Poems by T.S. Eliot
This selection, made by the preeminent critic Helen
Vendler, contains Eliot's most important early work. Here
in one volume is the poetry that so profoundly changed
American writing at the beginning of the 20th century.

READ THE TOP 20
SIGNET CLASSICS

1984 BY GEORGE ORWELL

ANIMAL FARM BY GEORGE ORWELL

FRANKENSTEIN BY MARY SHELLEY

THE INFERNO BY DANTE

BEOWULF (BURTON RAFFEL, TRANSLATOR)

HAMLET BY WILLIAM SHAKESPEARE

HEART OF DARKNESS & THE SECRET SHARER
   BY JOSEPH CONRAD

NARRATIVE OF THE LIFE OF FREDERICK DOUGLASS
   BY FREDERICK DOUGLASS

THE SCARLET LETTER BY NATHANIEL HAWTHORNE

NECTAR IN A SIEVE BY KAMALA MARKANDAYA

A TALE OF TWO CITIES BY CHARLES DICKENS

ALICE'S ADVENTURES IN WONDERLAND &
   THROUGH THE LOOKING GLASS BY LEWIS CARROLL

ROMEO AND JULIET BY WILLIAM SHAKESPEARE

ETHAN FROME BY EDITH WHARTON

A MIDSUMMER NIGHT'S DREAM BY WILLIAM SHAKESPEARE

MACBETH BY WILLIAM SHAKESPEARE

OTHELLO BY WILLIAM SHAKESPEARE

THE ADVENTURES OF HUCKLEBERRY FINN BY MARK TWAIN

ONE DAY IN THE LIFE OF IVAN DENISOVICH
   BY ALEXANDER SOLZHENITSYN

JANE EYRE BY CHARLOTTE BRONTË